Dear Parents, Let Not The Enemy Triumph Over Your Children

Dear Parents, Let Not The Enemy Triumph Over Your Children

YOLANDA THOMAS TAYLOR

Published by Spines
ISBN: 979-8-89691-131-9

Contents

Author: Yolanda Thomas Taylor

This book is designed to encourage every parent out there who has lost hope and given up on their children.

Just know that God is still in control.

Matthew 19:26b

> With man, this is impossible, but with God, all things are possible.

Dedication

I dedicate this book to every parent out there praying for their children's salvation and for their souls to be saved. Praying for the enemy to lose their lives and that God would free them from drugs, alcohol, homosexuality, lying, stealing, hate, transgender issues, murder, rape, and every other conspiracy that the enemy has tried to use to capture, cripple, stagnate, or even try to demise the lives of your children.

To the parents who have lost their children to hate crimes, suicide, accidents, drug abuse, murder, and the list goes on and on to the parents who feel as if there is no hope for their children, who feel like their children's lives are too far gone. The enemy has taken them so far out into the world that they see no way out for them. Today, I want to encourage you; there is not one human being in this world that the enemy has taken so far out that God is not able to deliver them.

No matter how dark a situation may seem, God is able to save your children. So do not lose hope because God knows when and how to pull them in. Parents don't give up and do not give in because help is on the way.

Psalm 127:3-5

Children are a heritage from the LORD, offspring a reward from him. Like arrows in the hands of a warrior, are children born in one's youth. Blessed is the man whose quiver is full of them. They will not be put to shame when they contend with their opponents in court.

In loving memory of Dale Murphy, Lester Thomas, and Gregory Thomas, gone too soon but will never be forgotten.

CHAPTER 1

Parents, your children are destined for purpose.

God created all humankind for his purpose. Believe it or not, we have always existed in the form of the spirit. God has a purpose for every one of your children here on earth. Every child arrived here on earth at God's appointed time. God chose their parents, siblings, and entire family. God knew their future even before they arrived here on earth. They were always a part of God's plan. God set their whole life up even before they were born. God knew who their parents would be, where they would live, what language they would speak, what lifestyle they would live, and what they would become in this earthly life. God had it all planned out even before they were conceived in their mother's womb. Every child has been chosen for God's unique purpose and plan. All children have been destined to fulfill a God-given purpose that God has placed on the inside of each one of them. They all carry something different; God has given each one of them a measure of strength, weakness, wisdom, knowledge, favor, hope, loyalty and understanding, but the list is much longer. Each child's ability is measured by their purpose. God has given them everything that they need to fulfill their God-given purpose here on earth.

Psalm 139:14

 Thank you for making me so wonderfully complex: Your workmanship is marvelous how well I know it.

It is God who created them; He knows everything about them. He knows their genetic makeup; he even knows the number of hairs on their heads. He knows their bone structure, blood type, and DNA. Parents, you must remember that it was God who created your children, and he knows all about them. He understands them, even when you do not. Parents, you must trust God with your children because he knows what is best for them.

God chose each one of your children before the foundation of the world. God always had your children in mind. God loves each of your children in such a unique way; He loves your children so much, and Satan is jealous of the love that God has for your children. Satan would do anything to destroy what God loves. Satan is after your children in so many ways. Satan does not care who or what he can use to bring destruction upon your children. Satan tells them it is okay to be rude, disrespectful, rebellious, and disobedient. He tells them it is okay to rebel against their parents and other adults. Satan always tries to come against God's plans for his people. He deceived Eve to go against God's will.

Genesis 3:1-4

> Now the serpent was more subtil than any beast of the field which the LORD God had made. And he said unto the woman, Ye shall not eat of every tree of the garden? And the woman said unto the serpent, we may eat of the fruit of the trees of the garden: But of the fruit of the tree, which is in the midst of the garden, God hath said, ye shall not eat of it, neither shall ye touch it, lest ye die. And the serpent said unto the woman, ye shall not surely die:

He has told your children that it is okay to live free and do whatever pleases them. He tells them it is okay to do drugs, pop pills, drink alcohol, become sexually active, and waste time on social media. Satan tries to challenge their minds; he wants them to believe that they can survive in this life, living any way they choose.

Proverbs 22:6

> Train up a child in the way he should go, and when he is old, he will not depart from it.

Parents, when you train your children up in God, even if they stray away, they will find their way back to God. But if you do not train your children in the LORD, then they have nothing to return to if they stray away. They are just left out there in the world, wandering, not knowing which way to turn. But if you trust God, he will always lead the way.

I Corinthians 10:13b

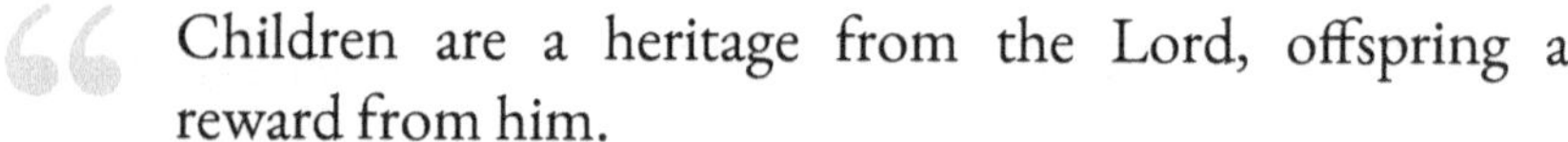 But God is faithful who will not suffer you to be tempted above that ye are able but will with the temptation also make a way to escape, that ye may be able to bear it.

God will always give your children a way to escape. Sometimes, God's way of escape does not meet your expectations as parents. Life is filled with choices, and your children do not always make the right choices. This is why it is so important that you, as parents, continue to keep your children before God daily because God hears your cry.

Psalm 127:3

Children are a heritage from the Lord, offspring a reward from him.

Parents, your children are a gift from God, and Satan is after your gifts. God chose you, and you, and you, to be their parents. Whether you were old enough, capable, or smart enough, it did not matter; God chose you. Because he knew you were the best parents for your children. God trusted their precious lives with you. It does not matter if you messed up; do not beat yourself up about it. Just ask God again and again to show you what to do and how to do it. Parenting is not an easy job if you do not believe me; just ask God, the one who fathers everything.

Whatever path your children take, it is all a part of their purpose and destiny. If they stray away, God knows how to bring them back to the right path. Parents, you must trust God through the process. Every path that your children take in life comes with a lesson, and it is up to them to learn the lessons.

Parents, you must try your best to help your children make the right decisions in life. Because, parents, you will not be by their side for every decision that they make. Parents, you know that your children want always to make the right decision. Sometimes, as parents, it is difficult to make the right decision when it comes to your children. But God will encourage and instruct you to do what must be done.

Proverbs 3:5-6

Trust in the LORD with all thine heart; and lean not unto thine own understanding, in all thy ways acknowledge him, and he shall direct thy paths.

There will come a time when you, as parents, will have to let go and let God. God is the most qualified when it comes to handling your children. God is the one who created them; He knows their genetic makeup. All your children are different; it does not matter how many children you have; they are all different.

God knows how much love they need; He knows their strengths, weaknesses, and their disappointments; he knows their likes and dislikes. God made each one of them in such a unique way, and he knows what to do for each of them. God knows their purpose and what they are destined to do. They are all purpose-driven by God.

Parents, every child will not take the same path in life. You can have five children, but they all will have a different purpose and destiny. Even if they get off track for a while, God knows how to rail them back into their original path. Every path that your children take in this life will not always be pleasing to you as parents. That is why it is so important, parents, that you continue to pray for your children and keep them before God daily.

There are no perfect parents; no matter how hard one tries; they will not always get it right. It is okay not to be a perfect parent because not being a perfect parent will always direct you back to God. When you do not know what to do, just turn to God; He has all the answers. Parents, you must see God in every situation and circumstance.

Romans 8:28a

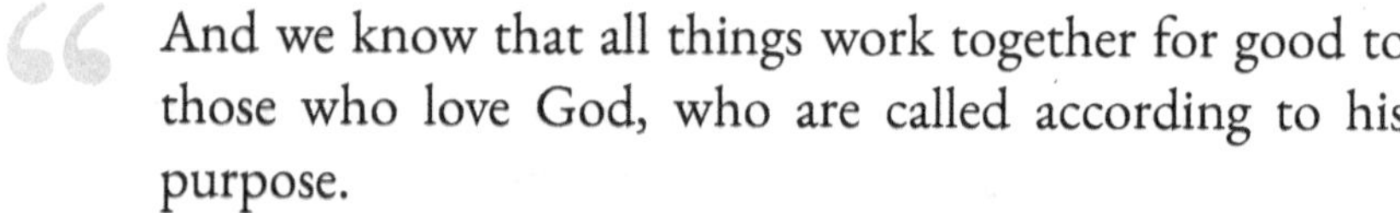

> And we know that all things work together for good to those who love God, who are called according to his purpose.

God did not say it would all be good and feel good, but he said it would all work together for your good. Parents, just trust God through the process because he knows what is best for your children. You must step aside and allow God to have his way in your children's lives. Children do not understand and see life as their parents do. Sometimes, as parents, you have to say no to things that your children ask to be involved in. Parents, you cannot love your children to the point that it is too hard for you to tell them no. Telling your children no can save their lives, keep them from being hurt, and wind up in places where they do not belong.

Even though you cannot protect them from everything, as parents, you wish that you could protect them every step of the way. God did not design it to be that way. Not one parent wants their children to take the wrong path in life. But one thing, as parents, you must remember is that God promised that he would never leave them nor forsake them, according to Hebrews 13:5. God has chosen each one of your children for a specific purpose. They all carry something great deep down on the inside of them. This is why it is so important that, as parents, you must be very careful what you call your children and what you say about their lives.

Proverbs 18:21

 Death and life are in the power of the tongue: And they that love it shall eat the fruit thereof.

If you tell your children that they are stupid or that they will never be anything in life, then they will begin to believe what you continue to say over their lives. If you tell them that they are smart and that they can be whatever they want to be in life, then they will believe that, and they may choose to set their standards higher, knowing that they do not have to settle for less. Sometimes, as parents, you struggle with the way you were raised, and you think that you should raise your children the same way your parents raised you. But when you learn to do better, you do better. If you want different results for your children, then you must do things differently. So, as parents if you do not like your outcome, you must break the cycle.

For example, suppose your grandmother, grandfather, mother, sister, brother, aunt, or uncle did not graduate from high school. In that case, someone in the family must break the cycle by graduating from high school and even taking it to the next level by going to college. Because generational cycles can be broken, you may have to work a little or a lot harder at it, but it can happen. This may mean that you will have to turn the TV off and take the cell phone and the video games away. Removing them from social media and letting them know This is how it's going to be done. These are the rules. You can make a planner and set goals for everyone in the household, and each person must reach their goal.

Believe it. You are teaching your children how to plan and set goals for themselves throughout life. But you must also include God in your plans and goals because, with God, your plans and goals will look a whole lot different than what you think. With God in your plans and goals, He will let you know when something is okay and when it's not okay. God will not leave you in this alone; He will be with you every step of the way, no matter what the outcome may be. You must learn how to trust God through the process.

Philippians 1:6

> Being confident of this very thing, that he which hath begun a good work in you will perform it until the day of Jesus Christ.

The very works that God has purposed on the inside of your children, God will work until it is completed. Sometimes, as parents, you get in the way of what God is doing in and through your children's lives. Parents want their children to meet their expectations in life; they want them to become what they want them to be in life and not what God has chosen for them to become in this life. Some parents want to make their unfulfilled dreams come alive in their children's lives. This can cause stress, difficulties, and chaos in your children's lives because, as parents, you are trying to mold them into something that they were never designed to be.

This type of behavior can bring on rebellion, disobedience, disrespect, unhappiness, anxiety, and the list goes on. As parents, you do your best in raising your children because you want what is best for them. That is why it is so important that, as parents, you must pray and ask God to lead and direct you in the lives of your children because all children are different. Children need balance in their lives, and as parents, it is your responsibility to help them balance life. With all the busy schedules in one household, there still must be a balance between parents working the children in school, homework, sports, activities, cooking, cleaning, grocery shopping, family time etc.

Life can become so busy with all the cares of the world, trying to juggle it all in one day. But you must stop and breathe, taking time to acknowledge God, the one who can help and teach you how to manage life in a much less stressful way. The first thing you must do is start your day off with God. Maybe a devotion with prayer, scripture, and a song; you will be surprised at how far it will take you throughout the day. It will help your day go smoother; it will give you strength, peace, and balance. It would help you focus throughout the day; all you must do is put God first.

Plan your day even if God makes some changes. Ask the Holy Spirit what it is that he has planned for the day and what His plans are for you. You would be surprised how the Holy Spirit would navigate your day, and the best part is you will not feel tired at all.

Philippians 4:13

I can do all things through Christ which strengthened me.

Especially to all the single parents who must juggle it all. Whether you are single or married, all need God to lead, guide, and direct their every move. When things get tough, he will see you through; no matter what happens, God will keep you balanced.

When you try to do things on your own, it can get messy, but if you keep God at the beginning, middle, and end, you will remain focused and stay on track because it is the Holy Spirit, that is leading you every step of the way. That is why it is so important that you teach your children to rely on God. Because once they reach a certain age, they think they know it all, and you cannot tell them anything. Parents, you must be prepared because when things get tough for them and trouble arises, the first one they will run to is you.

Raising children is not an easy job; believe me, it is a job. I am not talking about a nine-to-five where you clock in and out. It is a twenty-four-seven job where you never clock out. Parenting does not come with a time clock or a shift change; it is a lifestyle that you must live up to. When I was growing up, the elderly would always say, it takes a village to raise a child, even though parenting was much different back then. You did what your parents said you would do; you ate whatever they put in front of you on the table, and you wore what they brought you. And you better not say a mumbling word.

Parents now are dealing with a whole different breed of children. They think they can tell the parents what they are not going to do. Children must understand that life does not work that way.

> Children obey your parents in the Lord, for this is right. Honor your father and mother (which is the first commandment with promise;) That it may be well with thee, and thou mayest live long on the earth.

Parents, God wants you to teach your children how to have a long-lasting life here on earth by following his instructions. But if you are not teaching your children the word of God, then you cannot expect them to live out what they have not been taught. As parents, you must lead the way; you cannot be your children's friend; you must be their parents. Parents, you should not be doing what your children are doing; they should be doing what you are teaching them to do. Because if the head is out of order, so will the body be out of order. Parents, you must take your rightful place back by taking back your household and letting your children know that this is how things are going to be in this household. Parents, you cannot let the enemy triumph over your children. It is time that you step up and do it God's way and not your way.

Parents, you must not try to win the approval of your children when you have made a decision that involves them. God will give the parents instructions for the children. You know how, when one of your children wants to go out with their friends or sleep out, you have that strong feeling that you should tell them no? That is God letting you know it is not a good time to allow your child to do this. God speaks in so many ways. Your children may not be happy with your decision, but if you stick with the decision that God has given you, as time goes by, you will understand why he made that decision. Being obedient to God's decision can save your child's life.

Obedience is better than a sacrifice. There are so many things happening in the world today; you must trust God to protect your children. Whatever God allows, it is for his purpose and plans. You will not always understand God's purpose and plans for your children. Whatever God allows to happen in the lives of your children, only God knows the answer to that. You must trust Him and know that he is right even when you do not understand. Your children belong to God; they were always his. God loans them to you for a certain amount of time, but he never tells you how long. When they are born into your family, God knows the joy it will bring. They all come into this world with a purpose and plan from God. So, you must enjoy one another each day because no one knows God's plans.

Sometimes, this life can be complicated. It is like a jigsaw puzzle. When you think you have found that piece of the puzzle that looks like it is the perfect piece that fits, then you try to force it into that spot, but it does not fit. Why? Because it was never designed to fit into that spot. Sometimes, life becomes complicated because you are putting the pieces of the puzzle in the wrong place. Parents, you want your children to become what you want them to be. They come to you and tell you what they like and what they want to do. And you look at them as if they are crazy and have lost their minds. And you might say something like, why do you want to do that? That is not a good career; you cannot make any money doing that.

Instead of supporting their passion outwardly and secretly praying to God, ask him if this is what you want this child to do. Just because you don't see their vision does not mean that it will not work out for their good. If it is not what God has planned for them, then your prayers should be something like this. Lord, whatever your will is for this child, let your will be done. God, you created this child for your purpose and plans. God, I ask that you lead and guide my child every step of the way. In Jesus' name, I pray. Amen

Parents your children need to know how to make the right choices. So, if you allow your children to make some minor choices in the early part of their lives, as time progresses, allow them to make slightly more serious choices as they develop into their adolescence and young adulthood. By the time they reach adulthood, you can only hope that their better choice-making has developed with their growth. If you teach them to trust God in every choice that they make, I believe by the time they reach a certain age. They will know how to hear the voice of God.

Proverbs 3:5-6

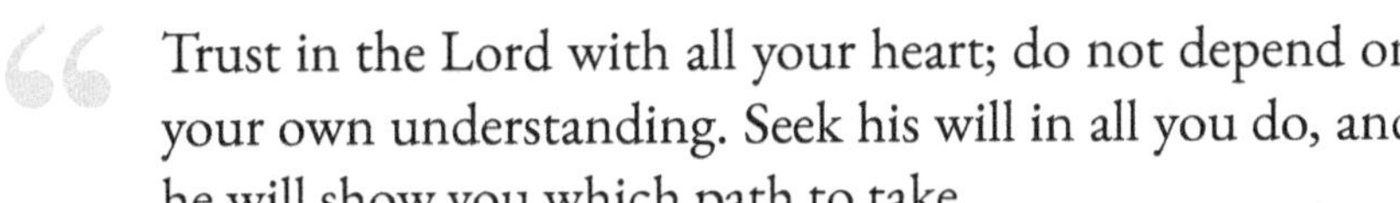

> Trust in the Lord with all your heart; do not depend on your own understanding. Seek his will in all you do, and he will show you which path to take.

Teaching your children the word of God is preparing them for the path of life. They must understand that it is God who leads, and they must follow his lead. As parents, your lives should be an example of what you are teaching your children. Your children must also understand that, as parents, you are not perfect, and you don't always get it right. Life is a learning process for both children and their parents; children teach their parents lessons, and parents teach their children lessons; you are all learning together. Being a parent is not easy; the struggle is real. You never know your children's next move or decision because they have a mind of their own. All you can do is give them to God and let Him work it out. Sometimes, your children's decision-making can bring trouble. Trouble is easy to get into but can be hard to get out of. It has been times when I would anoint my children's shoes, hats, and jackets and ask God to take care of them.

Psalm 121:1-2

 I will lift up mine eyes unto the hills, from whence cometh my help. My help cometh from the LORD, which made heaven and earth.

Parents, there will be times when you pray, and it seems as if things are getting worse; just know that God is working behind the scenes. God is in control of all things, even your children. So, regardless of what it looks like, hold your head up and keep on moving because God is in this with you. Parents, your children are vessels of God. I was told several times that your mess can become your ministry, and if you have never gone through anything, how can you help anybody? Life teaches your children lessons to help them grow and mature; without life lessons, they will remain the same. One thing I have learned about life is that it will keep on teaching you the same lessons until you learn and understand them: that's just life. Parents, you cannot hide your children from life lessons; one way or another, those life lessons will find them and teach them.

They are all just vessels designed for God's purpose and use, but God has left the choice up to them to whom they will yield their vessel. It is so important that they yield their vessel to the Holy Spirit because it is the Holy Spirit that will manifest through them. God gives the assignment to Jesus, and Jesus gives the assignment to your children, and the Holy Spirit manifests it through them. But only if they yield their vessel unto him. Parents, when you want something badly enough, what do you do? You pursue it until you get it. This is how your prayers must be for your children. You must pursue Almighty God to save your children so they will yield their vessels unto God. You must constantly bombard heaven on behalf of your children because you will not allow the enemy to triumph over your children.

James 5:16b

The effectual fervent prayer of a righteous man availeth much.

Parents, you cannot pray one prayer and think that everything is going to change. Prayer must become a lifestyle for you; your prayers must be consistent daily. It will not always be easy because there will be times when you do not want to get up at midnight or three o'clock in the morning when God wakes you up to pray. Sometimes, it will be a struggle; that is when you really need to push yourself to move because the enemy does not want you to pray for the very purpose for which God is waking you up. God will wake you up at certain times to do spiritual warfare on behalf of your children because he knows what Satan is plotting against them. You must cover them with your prayers and plead the blood of Jesus over them. The enemy wants to destroy your children; the bible tells us that the enemy comes to steal, to kill, and to destroy, but God came that we may have life more abundantly. John 10:10

CHAPTER 2

Destiny Calls

Parents, not all your children will be called to their destiny at the same time. But if they walk according to God's purpose and will, they will walk into their destiny at the appointed time, not a minute too late or a minute too soon, because when destiny calls, it will be God's timing and not their timing. That is why it is so important that you pray that God will lead and direct your children every step of the way. Parents, your children were created for God's purpose and destiny for their lives. That is why it is so important that you do not try to make your children become what you think they should be. God has given every one of your children a passion for what he has already purposed and destined for them to do. Many of them are already fulfilling their purpose and walking in their destiny without even knowing it.

 For my thoughts are not your thoughts neither are your ways saith the LORD. For as the heavens are higher than the earth, so are my ways higher than your ways and my thoughts than your thoughts.

Parents, just because your children's actions are not lining up with your way of thinking or your American dream for their lives does not mean that they are not fulfilling God's purpose for their lives. God saved Moses as a baby because he had a purpose for his life: to lead the children of Israel out of Egypt. He called Jeremiah at a young age to speak a prophetic word unto the nations. He called Esther to be a queen to King Ahasuerus to save the Jews when Haman plotted to kill them all. He called Rahab the harlot who married Salmon from the tribe of Judah and became the mother of Boaz. She was also one of the ancestors of Jesus.

So, parents, do not look at where your children are. Ask God to let you see them through his eyes. It is not about where they are in life right now, but it is where God is taking them in life. Did Moses' mother know that he was going to lead God's chosen people out of Egypt? Did Jeremiah's father know that he was going to be a prophet called to the nation at a young age? Did Easter's cousin Mordecai know that she would become queen and save the Jews? Did Rahab, the harlot, know that she would become King David's great-great-grand-mother and an ancestor of Jesus?

Parents, I know it does not always look right in your eyesight, but you must learn how to see your children through the lens of God. That is why it is so important that you pray over your children and ask God to lead and guide them every step of the way. Because God only knows where he is taking each one of them.

> For I know the thoughts that I think toward you, saith the LORD. Thoughts of peace, and not of evil, to give you an expected end.

Parents no matter what your children's lives may look like now, look deep within them, and see God's master plans for his/her life. God has called your children to fulfill a purpose here on earth. Even if you do not know or understand that purpose, just keep on seeking and trusting God. God will lead and guide your children down that path that he has chosen for them. God has chosen a different path for each of them; some things you may know, and some things you may not know are understand. But God had it all planned out before the foundation of the world. They all have a part to fulfill here on earth. But only God knows the length and time of their fulfillment here on earth. They all have an assignment here on earth. God is a God too wise to make a mistake. God never makes mistakes or accidentally does things. So never tell your children that they are a mistake or an accident.

God is the maker of all things and does everything with a plan and purpose behind it. So, parents, no matter how mad your children make you or how upset you feel, just take one look at them and say, God, no matter what, they are still a part of your plan and purpose. I know sometimes your children can work on your last nerve, but they are still God's chosen vessels, ordained and fit for his kingdom plans. Parents, you must also understand that just because God has chosen your children for his plans and purpose does not mean that Satan is not trying to stop them from fulfilling God's plans and purpose for their lives. Satan would do anything to take your children down that wrong path away from God's plans and purpose for their lives.

> The thief cometh not, but for to steal, and to kill, and to destroy I come that they might have life and that they might have it more abundantly.

Satan would do anything to trap your children. He would try to get them to see things his way and not God's way. Satan would try to take full control of their minds, how they think, act, and respond to life situations. He would try to fool them into thinking that their parents do not love or care about them. He would connect them with the wrong people in their lives. He would cause them to act out in a way that you never imagined. He would have them turn to the wrong people for advice instead of their parents' advice. Satan would try to use your children in any way he could. They will become disrespectful, disobedient, rude, angry, rebellious, selfish, and the list goes on. He would try to do anything to cause them to live a lie, and what I mean by that he would tell them that they are not good enough, that they are not beautiful or handsome enough. He wants them to believe that they are not enough. He tells them that they should change their appearance from whom God made them to be. He would convince them to leave home, turn to drugs, sell their bodies, drop out of school, and hurt themselves; he tells them all these negative things, trying to convince them that no one loves them.

Parents, I urge you to keep on praying for your children and never give up on them. This is what Satan wants you to do; he wants you to give up on them and kick them out so he can have his way with them and win them over for his kingdom. But we all know that Satan is a liar and the father of liars (John 8:44).

No matter what the situation looks like, no matter how far the enemy may think he has taken your children out into the world, you must remember that God is in control, and there is nothing too hard for God. Parents, you must keep in mind that God has his hands on your children, and no weapon that is formed against them shall prosper. Isaiah 54:17a.

Whatever it is that your children must face in this life, it will become their testimony. There are things that they all must face and go through in this life. But God promised you in Hebrews 13:5b that he will never leave them nor forsake them. Parents, you must remember that when destiny calls, God will lead your children to that correct path, and his plans and purpose will begin to unfold and blossom in their lives, and then you will know that God was with them all the time. Your children are a gift from God; He blessed you as their parents to play a huge part in their lives. Your job is to train them in the way that they should go, and when they grow old, they will not depart from it. Proverbs 22:6

I have heard so many parents say that children do not come with instructions. God has given you everything that you need in his word, including instructions for your children. If you do not know God's word, then you would always make the statement children do not come with instructions. All through the Bible, God gives you instructions for everything that pertains to life. The do's, don'ts, and so much more. It is up to you to seek God through his word and get to know him because as parents your children depend on you for everything.

Sometimes, when things do not turn out right for them, the first ones they blame are their parents; they really believe that it is the parents' fault. Parents, you must trust God even when you teach and train them according to God's word, and they still drift away. You have given them a solid foundation to return to. It makes a significant difference when you know that you have a God to return to. Life does not always seem fair, but when you know God's word, you can speak it over their lives daily, reminding God of his word.

Proverbs 18:21

 Death and life are in the power of the tongue, and those who love it shall eat the fruit thereof.

Parents, you have the power to speak into the lives of your children; it is never too late. Therefore, you must not allow the enemy to triumph over your children. It does not matter where your relationship with your children is; just keep on speaking God's word over their lives because you are reminding God of his word. God will make up the difference; He will bring balance into the relationship. Sometimes you may have to pray and speak God's word for a length of time, but God will answer at his own timing. In some cases, it may take days, weeks, months, or even years, but do not lose faith and trust in God because he knows what he is doing. Being a parent is not easy; it comes with headaches, heartaches, disappointments, struggles, and long-suffering, but God hears your cry. I always say the longer the struggle and the suffering, the greater the outcome. So, hang in there and do not give up because, in due season, God will come through for you. He hears your cries, he knows your struggles, and just when you want to give up and throwing in the towel, just know that your breakthrough is near. It is closer than you think.

Just know it want always to be this way; life comes with balance. Your children also bring joy and happiness into your lives. Having children is beautiful. They bring laughter, love, fun, humor, and lots of attitude, but they are God's given blessing. Within every child, there is ambition, drive, smartness, intelligence, uniqueness, boldness, and greatness. It is inside of them; with some of them, it just comes forth, and with some of them, you just must help them bring it out. Some may be shy, silly, funny, outgoing, dancers, joyful, happy, and playful. The enemy does not like the beauty of your children, the enemy will do all that he can to suppress the beauty within them. He would try to cover it up with pain, oppression, depression, and anxiety, and then the world put a title on it called mental health issues. Oh, but God. As parents, you must take another approach, see things differently from the world, and see your children through the lens of God. Parents, you must let your children know that greater is he that is in them, than he that is in the world. 1John4:4.

Your children possess great qualities of becoming doctors, lawyers, social workers, preachers, presidents, dentists, police officers, managers, CEO, dancers, construction workers, singers, poets, waitresses, waiters, pastors, cooks, evangelists, janitors, sanitation workers, prophets, prophetess, and the list goes on and on. All children take different paths in life, but God will get them to where he wants them to be. For your children to fulfill their purpose in life, they must allow God to lead them. Because they all have a different area in life to what they are called to. So, no matter where your children are in life, God has his people all over the world in all types of areas. God will meet your children where they are in life, and he will put people in their lives who will help them get where he wants them to be. Children come from all different types of backgrounds, and God has someone in every area in this walk of life. Parents, you may not know what area in life God has chosen, but you should know that when destiny calls, one must answer the call. Parents, you must trust God through the process. It does not matter what your children are faced with in this life. God is directing them every step of the way. It is not what they are going through in life. It is how they use what they are going through in life. Some children go through things, and it sends them into a place where they do not belong, and some children take what they go through and use it as a platform.

This is why it is so important that you encourage your children daily through the word of God. God's word has life; it is refreshing, renews, strengthens, motivates, restores, and builds you up.

Psalm 119:105

 Thy word is a lamp unto my feet and a light unto my path.

Teaching your children God's word is building a firm foundation in their lives. It teaches them how to trust God and look to Him for answers. God has the answers to every question in life. But it is your responsibility to teach your children God's word. Parents, you must help them make the right choices until they are able to do so for themselves. It is like teaching them how to walk; you want to let them go until you know that they are stable and can do it on their own.

Teaching them God's word does not mean they want to mess up or make mistakes in life. It does not mean that they want to stray away, but that solid foundation that is built on Jesus Christ, the living word, will always be in their hearts. God will always bring his word back to remembrance, and that way, they will always have a way to escape. God's word is transforming.

 For the word of God is quick, and powerful, and sharper than any two-edged sword, piercing even to the dividing asunder of soul and spirit, and of the joints and marrow, and is a discerner of the thoughts and intents of the heart.

That is how powerful God's word is. It would change your negative way of thinking and your bad attitude; it would even clean up your vocabulary. God's word is truth; it is filling their spiritual appetite. God's word is so powerful that it spoke everything into existence, which means your words carry power, so be careful what you speak over or into your children's lives. If you plant a seed and water daily with your words, it will grow into what you spoke into it. Parents and their children deal with a lot of things in this life. Sometimes, they do not always discuss these things with their parents; they hold them in. They are dealing with peer pressure, trying to fit in with the crowd, sex, drugs, school, an absent parent, and a lack of support. But God's word would make all the difference in their lives. God's word would help them cope with these issues. Knowing God would teach them that they are not in it all alone. They would know that the Holy Spirit is a comforter.

> Fear not, for I am with you; be not dismayed, for I am your God; I will strengthen you. I will help you; I will uphold you with my righteous right hand.

God's word gives principles for godly living. As parents, you must do your part and leave the rest to God. Parents, when your children hurt, you hurt, but you must trust God through the process. You must know that God is training your children for greatness. Training comes with lessons and responsibilities; God is teaching them how to cope with life. Your children will experience different things in life. It depends on their purpose, calling and destiny. Parents, I know it hurts to see them go through it, but you must come to a point in life where you must let go and let God. When destiny calls, they must answer. God will be with them for the rest of their lives. But there will come a time when God tests them all to see how they will handle the test. God knows when they are ready. God knows their weakness and their strengths. He also knows how much they can bear. He knows who is ready to listen. Some children mature faster than others, but God will get them all to their appointed place at the right time.

God wants what is best for them all. God does not just look at them and their potential; God knows their potential. God knows everything about them; He created them, and He knows just what he has placed inside of them. Life lessons help them grow and develop what God has placed inside of them. It is a process that does not happen overnight; it may take days, weeks, months, or years, but God will bring the best out of them. There will come a time when they must encourage themselves to get through the day. But the Holy Spirit will always be right there, bringing God's word back to their remembrance. The Holy Spirit will support them one hundred percent if they are walking in obedience to God's word. Being a child of God does not make life easy, but being a child of God makes life so much greater. Parents, you never know what tomorrow will bring, but what you do know is that God is faithful.

No matter what your next may be, God is in it with you. And just because you love your children does not mean that Satan want to try to attack you through them. When Satan cannot get to the parents, he will try to come after your children. He will make all kinds of attacks against your children just to throw you off track. He is cunning, crafty, conniving, scheming, and full of deceit. He will deceive your children to get involved in worldly things that you disapprove of. He would cause them to be disobedient, rebellious, and disrespectful, and he would even go as far as trying to bring embarrassment to you.

Parents do not give up on your children; it is all a trick of the enemy trying to get you to become frustrated with them. So, you can kick them out, and then he will try everything in his power to destroy them and rip your heart out with guilt. Parents do not allow Satan to triumph over your children. Keep on fighting for them through fasting, praying, and counseling. Seek God for direction; God will never lead you wrong and know that your prayers are not in vain. Even if children have left home, do not stop praying for them because your prayers are still a covering for them. No matter where they are in the world, God is everywhere, and so are His angels. God will put people in their lives who will help them, and they do not even know why those people are helping them. It is because their parents, family, friends, and church family are praying for them. No matter what they may endure in life, God will take those life-teaching lessons and allow them to help others on this journey. So, parents, do not beat yourselves up about the path that your children have taken; just remember God has it all under control.

Parents, I know it may seem as if all the responsibilities are on you.

You must go to your jobs where there is tumult, do the grocery shopping, do the cleaning, help with homework, take care of the children, pay bills, participate in activities, have quiet time with God, prepare dinner, and, last but not least, find time for yourselves. And this list can go on and on. These are just a few things that come along with parenting.

That is a true saying. One morning, as I was awakening from my sleep, I heard this voice speak to me, and it said, 'Comprende.' I said, "comprende." I said the word aloud, and I said, "I heard this word before," so I looked the word up and 'comprende,' which is a Spanish word that means to understand. Parents, God understands what you must endure. He knows all that you go through. Sometimes, you can learn your greatest lessons and training through the lives of your children. Parents, you must not forget that God has greatness on the inside of you too.

Parents can only parent their children with what they know. Each parent grew up in a different household and a different environment. Some had great parents, and some had not-so-great parents. Do not forget that every parent was once a child. The very way each child was raised when they grew up, they taught their children the same things they were taught. Think about it: when you grew up and had children, you cooked them the same meals your parents cooked for you. You trained them the same way you were trained. Some of the same things that your parents did with you as a child, you do some of those same things with your children. But in some families, some cycles need to be broken. Cycles that you should never pass down to your children. Each family is different, so, as parents, you must know which cycles in your family need to be broken.

There is no perfect family; every family has its flaws and shortcomings. Parents, you must take it all to God in prayer; he is a forgiving

God, and he wants you to come to him just the way you are. God is a deliverer. He knows how to heal past hurts and pain. So, you do not pass these negative things down to your children.

On the other hand, some families pass down good traits and healthy habits, but that does not mean they are a perfect family. No matter how great one may think that their family is, there is no perfect family. All parents need God to lead and guide them and their families. Some families suffer outwardly, while some families suffer silently. Either way, every family is dealing with something. I have heard this saying many times: hurting people hurts people. When you grew up hurting, you passed this hurt down to your children. If you do not recognize it and put a stop to it, it will go down from one generation to the next until someone in the family recognizes it and puts a stop to it by breaking the cycle. These generational cycles have been titled as generational curses, but God can deliver and set free.

John 8:36

> If the Son, therefore, shall make you free, ye shall be free indeed.

Parents, it does not matter what you want for your children in this life; you must put in the hard work, knowing that someday it will all pay off. Parents, never allow the enemy to make you feel like you have failed; that is why you must work extra hard. Because you are praying for God to lead and guide you as you lead and guide your children. You cannot walk through this life without God. If you feel as if you can make it through this life without God, you are living a false and empty life because, without God, you can do nothing. God is your source for all things that pertain to this life. Trying to live your life without God and believing that you are successful, because you have a nice house, car, job, big bank account, great friends, and a beautiful family. That is all good, but without God in your life, with all these things you will still feel empty and void. Parents, your children are trying to find their way in life, and they are looking to you for answers. That same God who chose you to be the parents of your children is the same God who chose them for his purpose. When destiny calls, one must answer: your children have so much greatness on the inside of them. If you do not help them to bring it out, Satan will do all that he can to suppress it down in them. Parents do not allow the enemy to triumph over your children. There is so much temptation out there in this world that seems good, but you know that it is the trick of the devil.

James 1:12

> Blessed is the man that endureth temptation: for when he is tried, he shall receive the crown of life, which the Lord hath promised to them that love him.

Parents your children must know how to fight along with you. If you do not teach them the word of God, then you are not teaching them how to win against the enemy. Parents, you must know that the battle is not yours or your children's; it is the Lord's. As parents, you must stand in the gap for your children until they are able to stand against the wiles of the devil. Your children are chosen to do great things in life, and the devil will do anything and everything to stop them from walking into their destiny. Every child has a calling on their life to do something. Some callings are greater than others; to know how great one's calling is, to know how great their suffering is. To be honest, not one parent on the face of this earth wants to see their children suffer. Parents will do whatever it takes to help their children to overcome any obstacles. But it will come a time when you must pray, and watch God work things out. For your children to get to the place where God wants them to be, they will have to endure some things in life. God never said that your children would be exempted from the trials and tribulations in life. Parents, I know you would love to step in and go through the storms of life for them, but life does not work that way. You must get out of the way and allow God to have his way in their lives. God does not allow your children to go through trouble to hinder or hurt them; he allows them to go through it to prepare them for their purpose and destiny. God use these things to strengthen them for what is ahead of them. God will never send them out unprepared because God knows what it would take to become all that he has chosen for them to become. God already has the gifts inside of them; they just need to be nourished, cultivated, activated, and loved. It is like a seed; you plant it and water it, and eventually, it will begin to grow and blossom into something great, beautiful, and flourishing.

Parents, when your children read and hear the word of God, it activates the gifts that God has inside of them. Their gifts become developed, skilled, nourished, and loved, and they come forth with greatness. You will see them blossom into what God has been preparing in them the whole time.

Preparation is not always easy; it can come with being let down by people, being overlooked, feeling isolated, lonely, mistreated, hurt, painful, frustrated, confused, and feeling lost and forgotten. But God has a purpose behind it all. When God has chosen you and destiny calls, you will answer no matter how life comes at you. Because when you are chosen for destiny, you will still find a way to rise above the pain. Those that are chosen are like a palm tree; no matter how tough the storm may be, that palm tree will bend, blow, suffer trauma, and even take some hard hits. But when the storm is over, the palm tree will stand tall and strong as if it has never been through anything. When the sun shines, the palm tree shines, and the beauty is still there. When

God has chosen your children, he has already given them everything they need.

Parents, as you continue to pray for your children, just trust God and see them as that palm tree, knowing that God will see them through the tough times. After all, they might tell you things like, you do not understand what I am going through, as if you have never been young before. Children think that their parents are old and outdated and have no clue what life all about is. Sometimes, your children will hold back on talking to you because they do not believe that you understand where they are in life. Some children are led to believe that their parents have this perfect life because this is what is being portrayed before them. This gives them a false perception of their parents. Children need to know the truth; they need to know that parents have problems, too. They need to know that parents are not perfect but are striving for perfection.

Titus 2:14

> Who gave himself for us, that he might redeem us from all iniquity, and purify unto himself a peculiar people, zealous of good works.

Children need to be reminded that their parents were once children and had to grow up with the pressures and temptations of life, too. I know that as the years go by, time changes, life shifts, people change, clothes change, music changes, and life itself can become a paradigm shift. Just because you are a parent does not mean that you are lost in society. Some parents keep up with the latest trends, along with everything else. Just because you are a parent does not mean you have lost touch with life. As parents, when your children cry, you comfort them; when they are sick, you care for them; when they are in trouble and have problems, you are right there with them, helping them to overcome it all. You are the same parent for whom they need to know and understand more than they give you credit. Children need to know that they do not have to take the world on alone because their parents do understand. They need to know that it is okay to turn to their parents for support and not just their friends.

Children seem to turn to their peers most often because they feel as if they can understand them better. Children see their peers as being on the same level as they are. They go through some of the same things in life; they spend time together, have some of the same friends, play video games together, talk on the phone, go places together, communicate on the same social media network, and go to football games together. And the list can go on and on, with reasons why they think that their peers understand them better. Parents your children need to know that with you, there is an open door where they can come in and express themselves and talk about anything and everything because parents understand, even though they do not hang out with them and their peers. They need to know that their parents love them no matter what is happening in their lives. God gives parents for a reason; parents are there to care for their children, provide for them, love them, teach them, motivate them, and encourage them. Parents are there for so many reasons. You do not get to choose your parents; God chooses them for you. God always gives you what you need and not what you want all the time. Therefore, children were not part of the choice when God chose their parents.

The parents that God chose for them may not give them everything that they need when destiny calls, but they can help them down that path of life. They will meet many types of people as they travel this path of life. Some will be there to help guide them on this path, and some will be there to try to throw them off this path. That is why the first eighteen years of their lives are spent with their parents; by then, they should have some stability on this path of life. So, when the enemy comes, they should be able to determine the difference. Not every child gets to receive the guidance of their parents. Life does not always take every child down that path with their parents in the first eighteen years of their life, helping them and preparing them for when destiny calls. Some children lose their parents and must live with other family members, while some children get to live with foster parents and go from one home to another. Some children get mistreated and have a hard life in the first eighteen years of their lives. You must remember that with God, there are no accidents or coincidences; whatever path God has each child take, it is for his purpose. Everything that God does, He has a purpose and a plan for it. God's ways are not our ways neither his thoughts our thoughts. Parents, you may see things from a natural point of view, but God sees things from a spiritual point of view. Why? Because God is a spirit, God does not allow children to suffer for no reason. There is a reason behind everything that a child goes through.

Every parent wants what is best for their children. The world paints this picture of how life should be. The world tells parents, this is how you should raise your children: you should send them to school for twelve years and then send them off to college for four years. This is what the world calls preparing your children for life, and once this is done, they tell you to send them off to live in this unforeseen world called life to pursue their careers, get married, and have a family of their own. This is what the world would call a good life, but not all children will get to take this path in life. Some will drop out of school and get kicked out of their parents' homes, some will leave home, some will go astray, and some will find their way. Why do you think these types of things happen to children? It is because each child has a different path in life. God already knows the path each child will take even before they start down that path called life. So, parents, do not get upset with your children if they do not take that beautiful path in life that you chose for them. Because it is not about your path of life for them, but it is about the path of life that God has chosen for them. When the time comes, destiny calls, and God is ready to use those children for His purpose, then you will see transformation take place in your children. Children are not here to become what their parents want them to become; they are here to become what God chose them to become. This is why it is so important that you do not allow the enemy to triumph over your children.

CHAPTER 3

Faith Walk

This life is a faith walk with God. What is faith? According to Hebrews 11:1, it tells us; Now faith is the substance of things hoped for, the evidence of things not seen.

This whole life is built on faith, whether we believe it or not. Does every parent have faith? Yes, whether they realize it or not, God has given every person a measure of faith.

For example, if you, as parents, allow your children to go out with their friends to the movies, then by faith, you believe that they will return home. Your faith can be activated even more by praying a prayer of faith over your children using the word of God. God's word will bring life to any situation if you use it and apply it to everyday living. Faith is believing that whatever you ask God, it will come to pass. You may not see it, but you are hoping and believing for it.

Parents, it does not matter where your children are in life. Just believe that God is right there with them. Even though they think they know everything and that they have it all together in life, parents just have faith and believe that God has them in the palm of his hand. Parents some children may be so far out into the world that it looks like there is no hope for them. It looks as if the devil has a hold on them, so do not give up; keep the faith and know that with God, all things are possible. God's timing is not on our watch. Parents, sometimes you can become very impatient with God's process, but you must trust the process because God knows what is best and what it will take to get them back on the right track. Parents, you love your children, but God loves them more and knows what is best for them. God knows what challenges they need in life to strengthen them for their purpose. No matter what they go through in life, God will not allow it to go to waste. God would take the good and the bad and make it all work together for their good. Having children takes a lot of patience because many parents would have given up a long time ago. They would have thrown in the towel and said, I quit, I give up, but God gave you enough faith to stay in the battle.

On this journey called life, you must have faith in God. Having faith in God is what keeps you grounded in hope because you are hoping and believing that God will turn your children's lives around for the better. It does not matter how many children you have; there will always be that one child who wants to test every nerve in your body. Sometimes, it seems as if the devil will try to push every button through them. Some children will keep you on your knees; that is why you must always pray in faith.

Mark 11:22

 And Jesus answering saith unto them, have faith in God.

On this faith walk, your children will have to face many challenges, but God will be right there with them every step of the way. When they want to give up and quit their dreams because it seems as if nothing is going the way they planned, it is an opportunity for God to get their attention and to bring their focus back to him. There will come a time in life when God steps in and says, my child, I have a greater plan for your life, but you must have faith and believe that I have already worked it out for you. Parents, it is times like these when God would use these difficult times to test your faith because walking with God requires faith. Children want always see life the way their parents see it. God would show parents things because God knows that children are not mature enough to understand. Children get upset with their parents because they tell them what they cannot do. Parents, it is okay to say no to your children even when you do not understand. But you know that something inside of you is telling you to say no. He is called the Holy Spirit; the world would say it is your intuition, but you know better.

Psalm 127:3

 Children are a gift from the Lord; they are a reward from him.

Children are a blessing; they are placed in your lives for a reason. Children do not get to choose their parents, and parents do not get to choose their children. God knows what is best for each child; He knows what they need and who they need. Children do not always get the best of parents, and parents do not always get the best of children, but God has a purpose behind it all. Some children grow up in households where things are rough. Do they stop living? No, they continue this faith walk. Greatness is sometimes built on struggles and tough times because God knows how to bring the best out of your children. As parents, you raise your children the best that you know how. But the truth be told, you do not know who you are raising. God has chosen so many children to do many great things for his kingdom. It is the parent's responsibility to lead and guide them the best that they know how. Children do not always follow the leadership of their parents. They want to follow their friends, they rebel, and they do not want to listen; they become disrespectful. But do not give up parents; keep the faith because God is working behind the scenes. One day, you will look back and say, God has brought my child a long way. Children go through things in life also; it is not always easy for them, but it is all for the purpose of God. This journey is a faith walk.

2 Corinthians 5:7

 For we walk by faith and not by sight.

Parents, you must walk by not what you see but by what you do not see and still yet believe. God is faithful; He is a God who cannot lie and will not lie. How children are raised and what they have experienced in life help to prepare them for this journey called life. Life can bring on a lot of things; it can bring trouble, sorrow, discouragement, disappointments, happiness, joy, peace, and victories. You never know where life is going to take you. Children experience many things in life because they are human beings trying to find their way. Children are so incredible; they are full of humor, laughter, fun, and joy. They cry, pout, act stubborn, and want to have everything their way. Isn't that just like the average human being? Each generation has a future generation of children, and that is why it is so important, parents, that you do not allow the enemy to triumph over your children. Because they are the future, and God has greatness inside of them. There is a champion on the inside of them called the Holy Spirit; He knows how to bring out the best in them.

Children are great achievers; they are gifted, anointed, talented, creative, and amazing. They all have something special that has been given to them by God; who knows how amazing they are. Even if their lives take a turn for the worse, that amazing gift is still on the inside of them. Wherever they go, that amazing gift and purpose remain with them. God preserves it and keeps it because only God knows how to bring to pass what he has purposed on the inside of them.

Philippians 1:6

> Being confident of this very thing, that he which hath begun a good work in you will perform it until the day of Jesus Christ.

Children are very valuable human beings created in the image of God for his purpose and use. Parents, when you raise your children in a household, teaching them the word of God will become rooted and grounded in their lives. If your children grow up and leave home and go about their business doing their own thing in life and things become complicated for them, they will always have God to turn back to. God will direct them back to that straight and narrow path to him. Oppose if your children do not know God or have a relationship with him, where will they turn? If they do not know that they can turn to God, then they will turn to other people and other sources. But if you train them up in God, they will always know that he will accept them with open arms. Parents, Satan is out there waiting for the first opportunity that he can get to try and destroy your children. This is why it is so important that you pray in faith and believe that God will guide them every step of the way on this faith walk. Parents, it does not matter how many children you have God can handle them all. The word of God says many are called, but few are chosen. If you have five children, they are all special to God, no doubt, but there is always that one child that you look at and notice that there is something special about that child. God has many chosen vessels in families. (Paraphrasing) 1 Samuel 16, Samuel the prophet went to Jesse's house to anoint his son king as God ordered him to do. Jesse brought his sons to pass before Samuel, but God told Samuel not these. So, Samuel asked Jesse, "Are these all the sons that you have, Jesse said I have a younger son, and he is tending to the sheep. Samuel asked Jesse to send for him, and when David arrived, God confirmed with Samuel that he was the chosen one, and Samuel anointed David with a horn of oil. Although Jesse had eight sons, according to the bible, David was the chosen one in the family. David was chosen to be king over the children of Israel, God's chosen people. So, parents, never underestimate the power of God because you just may have a chosen seed among you, and you do not even know it.

Most chosen children usually have a tough life because a lot of people look at them and say that there is something special about them. Everybody often picks on chosen children. Genesis 21:9 tells how one day, Ishmael, whom Hagar the Egyptian had born to Abraham, was playing with Sarah's son Isaac. What was happening here was that Ishmael began to mock Isaac to the point of persecution, and Sarah, Isaac's mother, noticed what was taking place and asked her husband Abraham to send them away. Parents, you see, Isaac was the chosen one, and just like Sarah, you too must protect the chosen one that God has given unto you. Parents, stop just viewing your children as if they are existing human beings and see them through the eyes of God. Because on this faith walk, there will be trials, tribulations, and storms, but God promised that he will never leave you nor forsake you (Deuteronomy 31:6).

No matter what they face in this life, they must remember that they are destined for God's purpose and plan. Parents have difficult times in life when children are growing up; they are trying to figure out who they are and what they want to become. On this journey called life, children will take different paths and travel down different roads, seeking a place to belong. They know that they are in search of something, but they are not sure what that something is. The more support a child receives from family and loved ones, the greater the chance that the child will find something they are looking for. Family support makes a huge difference in a child's life; the more support that child knows he or she has, the harder they will try. They would give life all they have, and with God on their side, leading and guiding them through. They will be able to overcome the obstacles, the rough times, and the rocky roads ahead, and before you know it, they will be on top doing what they were chosen to do. Life does not turn out the same for every child because every child has a different purpose. Some children live long lives, while some live shorter lives, but either way it goes, they all have a purpose to fulfill.

Behind every child's life, there is a God-given purpose, and that is why it is so important that each child receives the support that they need on this faith walk. Parents let not the enemy triumph over your children. Love them, pray for them, and speak positive affirmations over their lives every day. No matter what direction their lives are headed in, speak positivity over their lives, because the word of God carries power.

Proverbs 18:21

> Death and life are in the power of the tongue: and they
> that love it shall eat the fruit thereof.

Parents, be careful what you call your children because if you tell your children every day that they are dumb guests what, they will believe it and will become dumb why because you spoke it into existence. There is power in your tongue. Positive affirmations can give your children more courage and hope. It would make them strive harder and become go-getters. Parents, a life filled with love, will be life-givers of love, so parents watch your tongue because it carries powers. The more a parent talks down to their children, the easier the access is for the enemy to take them down the wrong path in life. Never make your children feel like they must turn to the world for support because the world is filled with a lot of unwanted support. This is what happens when children cry out for love and attention. Children should never have to fight for the love and attention of their parents because their parents should be their support system. Be mindful that some children are not as strong as others. Some children are very sensitive and fragile, and your words can either make or break them.

Colossians 4:6

> Let your speech be always with grace, seasoned with salt,
> that ye may know how ye ought to answer every man.

Parents, it is our responsibility to bring this generation, and every generation to come, back to God. Children are turning to everything in the world except for God. They run to video games, drugs, alcohol, tobacco, sex, clothes, shoes, money, social media, and gender confusion. The reason children are turning to these things is that they do not know God. Every household is not teaching the word of God or showing the love of God to their children. Families no longer sit together and have dinner; the communication barrier has been broken down in families. The enemy has come in and separated the family. Daddy is sitting in the recliner watching sports, Momma is on the phone with her girlfriend, and the children are playing crazy, killing video games, talking on the phone, on social media, watching pornography, having sex, getting high with their friends, or out doing other things that they have no business doing. Children in the household act as if they oversee the parents, telling the parents what they are not going to do. Children have gotten to the point that they do not want to do chores anymore, and they do not have to. Why? Because no firm authority figures are telling them what they are going to do.

It is time for the parents to step up and take their rightful place in the home. Children all over the world are crying out for their parents' love and attention. Parents, you cannot give your children stuff and think that is the answer for them; children need their parents' time, love, and attention. Parents are so busy out there in the world grinding and getting their hustle on while their children are dying right before their eyes. Parents let not the enemy triumph over your children. This faith walk may be a bit tough, but with the help of God, He will see you through. I challenge you to give God a chance, and I guarantee you he will work out your situation his way.

 Trust in the LORD with all thine heart and lean not unto thine own understanding. In all thy ways acknowledge him, and he shall direct thy paths.

Parents, when you have done all that you know how to do, just lay it at the altar before God. God wants you to come to Him with every situation and circumstance. Living a life for God does not mean life will always be easy because it will not. There will be times of trials and tribulations, but the greatest thing about this is that God will hold your hand through it all. He will see you through it. God is a perfect God; he makes no mistakes. Whatever God allows your children to go through, He always has a plan for it. God would never do anything to hurt your children; if anything, He would do whatever it takes to help them. Children come in all sizes and ages; there are infants, toddlers, youths, young adults, and adult children. It does not matter how old they are; you will still call them your babies. Parents, which means children of all ages, need prayers because the enemy does not care how old they are; Satan would do anything to try and destroy them. Children are special in the sight of God, and God loves them with all their shortcomings. God knows their every thought and move; God knows what they are going to do even before they do it. God even knows the outcome of every situation. Parents, sometimes it is heartbreaking when God says it is time to let them go so, they can grow and develop into the person that he called them to become. Parents, be honest with yourselves; you know that you can look at some of your children and say they are not ready. Do you think that God does not know that? God knows everything about your children; He even knows things that you do not know about your children because God created them, and He knows all about them.

Parents, when you see how painful it is to let them go, God sees how great that child will become for Him and the glory they will bring to Him. God is so amazing; He never sees things the way you do. God sees their future when parents only see their present moments. God's way for them is so much greater. Do you have that one child who gave you the toughest time in life, and you did not know what was going to become of them? But one day, God got a hold of them and turned their entire life around for the better. Now you look at that child and say, I know there is a God because only God could have changed my child's life. Maybe it was to make a believer out of someone; you just never know what your children are called to do. Parents, God does things on purpose to better one's life and never to hurt anyone.

Ephesians 2:10

> We have become his poetry, a re-created people that will fulfill the destiny he has given each of us, for we are joined to Jesus, the anointed one. Even before we were born, God planned our destiny and the good works we would do to fulfill it!

Parents, if you give your children to God, you will be so amazed at what God would do through them. Look at it this way: they are citizens of the kingdom of God, and earth is a temporary assignment. The assignment was given by God to be fulfilled here on earth. The best example I can give is the life of Jesus. Jesus came to earth for the purpose of dying for the sins of the people, but on his way to his purpose, he was given many assignments. That would help to prepare him for his purpose of dying on the cross for the sins of the entire world and reconciling the world back to God. There will be many assignments and life lessons on this journey, but God has a purpose for it all. On this faith walk, your children will encounter many things, but remember they are not alone; God is right there, holding their hand, taking them step by step until they discover their passion, that thing or things they love to do. All children have a passion for something. Once their passion is discovered, they will become a blessing to many people. Their passion will bring them to many assignments; it depends on the length of time that God has given. Some assignments last longer than others, but it depends on what God has in mind.

Every assignment is a faith walk; children are destined for the things that God has planned for their lives. In the same way, parents teach their children from infancy to adult life; this is how God must teach and train their spiritual lives. Some children accept Jesus as their personal Lord and Savior at an early age and begin their teaching and training in the Lord. While some children have no idea what it means to be taught about God because there is no upbringing about God in their household. Therefore, some children grow up and learn about God from other people, friends, tough times, troubles, and so on. God has a way of reaching them. Sometimes, I just sit back and think, and I say life is like a jigsaw puzzle.

You try to put pieces into places where they do not belong. It looks as if it is the perfect fit, and, in your mind, you believe that it should fit, but it does not. That is what children do; they try to fit in where they do not belong, and they believe that they belong there. Because the group of friends they hang out with fit in just fine. They do not understand why they do not fit in where their friends are. Until they get to know Jesus as their personal Lord and Savior, they will never know that they fit in on the other side of the puzzle. In Jesus is where they would find their right fit. It is like this: if God called one child to sing in the choir, another to dance, another to teach, and another to pray. If the child who sings wants to teach, the child who dances wants to sing, and the child who prays wants to dance, then the puzzle will be incomplete because everyone is in the wrong place.

46

All children have been called and chosen for something; they must seek God, and this is where they will notice that they have a passion for what they are supposed to be doing. Life has a way of taking people down many roads to get them to the right place where they fit. God is the orchestrator of all things, including the lives of your children. When they take a wrong turn in life, God knows how to put them back on the right track. Life can be a little tricky because, as parents, you may think that you have it all figured out and God turns and goes left on you, but do not worry, God is controlling their destiny. Parents, you want your children to have a perfect life, but you must remember that God loaned them to you for you to help them down this path called life, and at some point, you will have to let them go and allow God to have full control. For some parents, that can be very difficult to do, because it is hard to let go of your grown babies, who are full grown adults. The time will come, parents, when you will have to let them learn life lessons on their own. There may be times when they come back and ask for your advice, and I am sure you will give them the best advice you can give them, but you must let them figure it out on their own. And when they do, they will come back and thank you for making it tough for them because if you had not, they would not have learned the things they did. Parents, growth comes with pain and failure in this life, but the greatest part about it is they do not have to go through it alone. God is right there by their side, leading them every step of the way. God will never lead them down a road of destruction, but he will guide them off that road that road of destruction to that straight and narrow path. God wants nothing but the best for them, but they must also do their part by obeying God's word.

Obedience brings about great blessings. Parents think about that obedient child who does all that you ask, and they even go above and beyond to do nice things. It just melts your heart and makes you do so much more for them. God feels the same way about His children when they do it with love and a smile on their faces. Obeying God's commandments, he rewards them greatly, and there is nothing God will not do for his children when they walk obediently to his word. On this faith walk, obedience plays a big part because when God gives instructions, one must obey and follow through with God's request. Parents your children will not stay toddlers or youths forever; therefore, it is very important to teach them how to obey God through his word. So, when they grow up, the word of God will not depart from them. Even if they wander off in life, they will find their way back because God's word is rooted and grounded in them. On this faith walk, without God, it would be like a fish trying to survive out of water. On this journey called life, it will require some faith. Parents, sometimes children are afraid to do certain things, but if you encourage them and tell them that they can do it, guess what? They will believe that they can. Helping their belief will strengthen their faith. When reading the word of God, you believe it, speak it, act on it, and by faith, believe what it says will come to pass.

Young children's brains are like a sponge; they absorb things fast and easily. Before you know it, they will be saying what you say. So, watch your words and be careful of what you are teaching them because they are soaking it all up. Teaching them about faith at a young age, they will absorb it, and as they grow and develop in life it will become more and more activated in their life.

James 2:26

> For as the body without the spirit is dead, so faith without work is dead also.

On this faith walk, they must activate their faith to overcome trials and tribulations. Through faith, God will see them through. God already knows what they need; they must believe that they can have what they say. On this faith walk, they will encounter many things in life, but they must prepare themselves for the battle. Parents, your children need your prayers; do not allow the enemy to triumph over your children. It will not always be easy because life can be a struggle, but you keep pressing through the process. Children do not always understand the process, so it is very important for the parents to stand in the gap for them until they learn to do it for themselves. Parents, your children do not see the battle; they just go through life unbothered and unlearned by the tactics of Satan. Therefore, he will try to use your children to get to you, to throw you off course, for him to gain victory over your children. This is why prayer is so important: when you pray and give it to God, he will handle every situation. God does not always handle things the way we think he should, but he always handles them far greater than you could ever imagine. Without God, things would be impossible to handle, but with God, all things are possible (Matthew 19:26). Parents, when you pray, pray God's word because God will stand behind his word. God will not and cannot lie; His word is truth. That is why studying and knowing God's word is so important. Try to memorize one scripture every week, and before you know it, the scripture will flow naturally in your prayers.

Paying in faith will change things. Children are a great responsibility; as parents, you do not only care for their physical being, but you must also care for their spiritual man. Children will someday grow up and become adults, and how you train them from childhood will make a difference in their adult lives. Training them at an early age will help them make better choices and decisions when their parents are not around. Parents training them up in the Lord would make a significant impact on their lives. Children want the guidance and teaching of their parents, along with their attention. It shows them how much you love and care for them. Children need to know that their parents love, care for, and support them. Because life alone can be an everyday challenge, parents should pray for their children and teach them how to speak positive affirmations over their lives. It is never too early or too late to learn the power of prayer and words. Everything that God created, He spoke into existence; words carry power, and there is power in praying the word of God. What you speak into the universe is what the universe will give you in return. God said, let there be light, and the light came forth. God spoke into the universe, and the universe gave Him what He asked for. This is how powerful your words are, so be careful of the words that you speak over your children. Because whatever you call them will become stored in their memory. So, parents, remember that words can hurt. They can also bring joy, happiness, and encouragement, so choose your words wisely.

Think about that time when your children were toddlers and when you first told them "No" that they could not have something. What type of effect did the word "no" have on them? Did they cry, scream, fall out, or did they throw a temper tantrum? Do you see what a two-letter word can do? It can cause some chaos, but it is okay because there will be many times when you must tell your children throughout life "no." A small two-letter word no can save your children's lives. Children want always to understand their parent's answers, but they will always remember your harsh words toward them.

Parents, if you tell your children to be kind, listen and be nice, but if you are not saying kind things or being nice to them, how would you expect them to know how to do or say positive things to others? Parents, your words will go a long way, so be careful what words you put out into the universe over your children. On this faith walk, your children will learn many things, good and bad, but they need to know that they have a choice. Parents, positive affirmations spoken over your children can help them to make the right choices. If you speak to your children every day, they will make the right choice, choose great friends, and so on. Eventually, the universe will give you what you ask. Parents continue to speak and teach positive affirmations to your children, and one day, you will see it all unfold. Parents must speak positive affirmations over their lives so they can continue to encourage their children, and parents are not surprised when their children start to speak their positive affirmations over themselves and others. Children do and say what they see and hear. Children do not know how to raise themselves, so they depend totally on their parents for everything. Parents, their precious lives are in your hands; what you instill in them is what you are going to get out of them. Parents, your children will not always be under your wings, but they will forever be in your prayers.

CHAPTER 4

Learned Behaviors

Many things can be learned behaviors; it can be something as simple as learning how to eat, walk, or talk. Learned behaviors can be taught; learning to read a book for thirty minutes a day will become a learned behavior. So, parents teaching their children how to pray, read the Bible, and speak positive affirmations daily can lead to learned behaviors. Children's learned behaviors can be positive or negative, depending on what they are being taught. Parents your children can learn to be as great as you allow them to become. All children are gifted differently; they all have a different purpose in life. Children must learn who they are, and that may take some time. Truth be told, we all operate through learned behaviors.

For example, your parents learned how to do things the way their parents did; they never asked why you did it this way or that way; they just did whatever their parents did. Then your parents taught those very same things to you, and you never asked why it was done this way; you just did whatever it was that your parents taught you. The only reason you did it was that it was what you were taught. It is called learned behavior. Parents, it is okay to change your style of teaching;

you learned that some things you were taught were incorrect. And now you have that big opportunity to teach your children the correct way. Parents, life is a learning experience; you learn as you go through various things in life. Life will teach you many lessons; there are so many types of learned behaviors, but I want to talk about learned behaviors that will help children grow and blossom into the person whom God has called them to be. When children are born, they are innocent; they do not know much of anything at this point, but it is up to the parents to teach their children good, learned behavior. Children learn who their parents and siblings are, along with other family members. Children can also learn who God is through the teachings of their parents.

Children are like sponges; they soak up everything, and they learn so fast until you reach a point where you say, I must be careful what I say in front of these children because children will begin to repeat what they hear and what they are being taught. Reading the bible to your children, along with other books, will help develop their minds, and they will begin to ask many questions. Parents, you must be ready to give them the answers. Parents of young children will ask them a question, and you give them the answer, and they will come back and ask you, why? They want an explanation for your answer. Teaching children is extremely critical because these learned behaviors will follow them throughout life, yes, even into their adult life. God's word is filled with many godly principles, dos, and don'ts; God's word is filled with instructions, wisdom, and knowledge. It teaches obedience, love, forgiveness, kindness, respect, gentleness, and compassion. It also teaches about the life of disobedience, disrespect, unforgiveness, unlove, hate, and the list goes on. But they all come with different rewards; these are all learned behaviors, whether they are good or bad. Parents play a vital role in correcting these behaviors when they are not good and encouraging those behaviors when they are good. This will help your children understand the difference between right and wrong.

So, when your children are in the presence of other children, and they must decide if it's okay to do or say certain things that other children say and do, learned behaviors can also be taught outside of the household as well.

That's why it's so important for parents to monitor the company that their children entertain. Being in a good community does not mean that your children are in good surroundings of company. Every household upbringing is different; as parents, you usually know the difference. For some children, being in good company can teach them good, learned behavior and vices versa, whereas being in bad company can teach them bad, learned behavior also.

Proverbs 22:6

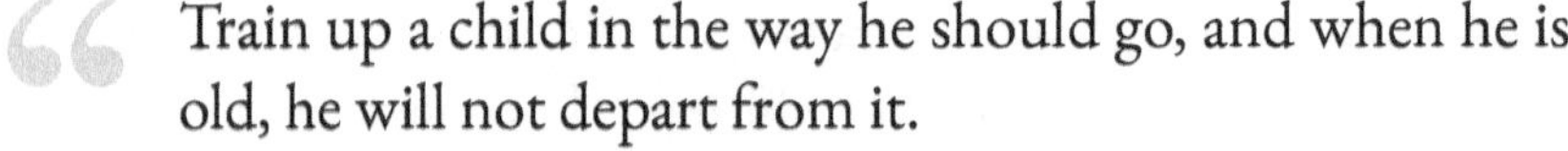

> Train up a child in the way he should go, and when he is old, he will not depart from it.

The older your children become, the less they will be under their parents' influence. They will be in the same home as their parents, but they will be doing something different in another part of the home. They may be in their room doing homework, listening to music, playing video games, on their cell phones, or reading a book. Most children tend to do the things that they are taught to do and are allowed to do. If you read the bible to your children while they are growing up, eventually, your children will start reading the bible on their own. Children do and say what they see and hear; parents are the most influential people in their children's lives. So, most of your children's learned behaviors come from home and then from school. Children can learn both negative and positive behaviors from home and school. As parents, when you recognize negative behavior, you must discipline your children right away.

Proverbs 23:13-14

 Do not hesitate to discipline a child. If you spank him, he will not die. Spank him yourself, and you will save his soul from hell.

Parents, you don't have to be afraid to correct your children; correction will help them move in the right direction. As children grow older, they want to make their own choices and decisions, some of which are good and some not so good. Parents, when their choices and decisions are good, let them know you appreciate them for making the right choice and decision, and vice versa. When they make bad choices and decisions, let them know that you disapprove of the choice and bad decision that they made. Parents, you must let them know so they don't make the same mistakes again. All children are different; some are easy to talk to, and they will listen, and some children will not listen to avoid the same mistakes. So, parents, no matter what the case maybe, you must keep on parenting them, because some children learn differently than others. Sometimes, being a parent can really be tough, but you must keep on praying and trusting God to see you through it all and know that you can do all things through Christ, which strengthens you Philippians 4:13.

Children are beautiful to have; they can bring joy and happiness into your life, but you must still be their parents and not their friends. If God wanted children to be on the same level as their parents, then there would be no need for parents. In some households, there are two parents, a single parent, grandparents, aunt, or uncle, that are in authority over that household, and those children must obey their authority, or there will be consequences if they refuse to obey their authority. Parents, do not think for one minute that the devil will not rise in your children, causing them to disobey you, but you must take authority over the enemy.

Ephesians 6:12

 For we wrestle not against flesh and blood, but against principalities, against powers, against the rulers of the darkness of this world, against spiritual wickedness in high places.

Parents let not the enemy triumph over your children. God gave parents authority over the children; He did not give the children authority over the parents.

Ephesians 6:6

 Children, obey your parents in the Lord; for this is right.

Even though there are two parents in the household, a mother and a father, there are different authorities in that household. If you notice, when the father speaks, he just gives a certain look, and the children's whole demeanor changes quickly; as opposed to if the mother speaks, she must tell the children repeatedly before they even move unless they know momma is not playing today. With a father there are no days like this; there is just something about a father's tone of voice; it speaks with volume, and children just fall in line. Children look up to their parents, and they learn both positive and negative aspects from them.

True story: I knew a man that I used to work with; he had a beautiful wife and daughter. The man started to take an interest in one of the other coworkers. So, I asked the man why he was cheating on his wife with that woman, knowing that he was a married man. The man told me, my daddy left my mom and his children for another woman, so he will do the same thing that his daddy did to him and his family. This is what you would call a learned negative behavior. Even though the young man decided to do what his daddy did, I hope that one of the parents sits the young man down and explains to him the consequences of adultery. Because if not, this young man will go through life thinking that he can treat women this way. If the young man had known the word of God, he would have understood how he was supposed to love his wife.

Ephesians 5:25

 Husbands love your wives as Christ loved the church and gave himself up for her.

Teaching your children the word of God is a positive learned behavior; it will stir them in the right direction. Being a parent is not easy because parents were once children themselves, and they also learned positive and negative behaviors. However, somewhere down the line, you as parents have to say, this is not right, and it will go no further, and decide that you will not teach those behaviors to your children or generations to come. A negative upbringing can cause a negative household, which can create tumult and chaos in the lives of your children. Learned behaviors will follow an individual for the rest of their life until the individual decides to make changes to their life. Not all learned behaviors are negative and require no change; it is up to the individual to recognize the negative behavior to make any changes. Can you imagine a child being allowed to throw a temper tantrum, act stubbornly, be selfish, not taught to share, or not shown any love? What happens if these negative learned behaviors are not corrected? They would follow the individual into adulthood, where there would be problems and consequences. Not every individual was raised that way, so they will not understand your problems; neither will they care to understand your problems.

For example, as your children grow into adults with negative learned behaviors and enter the workforce, if their boss asks them to do something that they do not want to do, they start to pout and throw a temper tantrum. Now, they must face the consequences by going into the boss's office either for a verbal or written warning. Parents, you can spoil your children, but the world will not accept your spoiled adult children. The world will not care about your children's upbringing. When your adult children enter the workforce, they will expect them to act like grown, mature adults. Every child has been raised in a different type of environment; some children had it hard, and some children had it easier. Some children had to deal with the hurt and pain that was brought on by childhood trauma, which may have caused anxiety, depression, oppression, bipolar disorder, and many other disorders. But it does not mean that they cannot function in the real world or the workplace. While some children were brought up in a better environment where they had a better support system that gave them the help they needed to thrive in life, when they become adults, they have more confidence and can focus much better. However, they may have an attitude problem, or they may be rude, arrogant, selfish, or spoiled due to their learned behaviors. Parents are not perfect, but there are so many ways the enemy would try to triumph over your children.

Through broken homes, one parent may be trying to do it alone. Divorce can also cause some children to react in a rebellious way, which can lead them to pick up learned behaviors outside of the home. The enemy would use these outside learned behaviors to disrupt the household. So, not all learned behaviors that are brought into the workforce are part of the individual's upbringing. Sometimes, life can seem complicated, but it is still operational. Parents know that their children are fully grown adults and have moved on with their lives, so it is time for them to be the adult that carries more responsibility that requires them to work on their own.

> When I was a child, I spoke as a child, I understood as a child, I thought as a child; but when I became a man, I put away childish things.

You cannot raise an adult all over again; those behaviors will go on with them into adulthood. Some learned behaviors can cause some serious problems in adulthood. It does not matter how gifted, smart, or talented you may be; the elders will tell you your gifts can take you places where your character cannot keep you. Do not allow bad learned behaviors to ruin your children's adult life. Parents teaching their children good, learned behaviors will help them in the long run; it will teach them how to conduct themselves in a manageable and respectable way. Bad learned behaviors can cause tough disciplinary actions in their adult life, which can lead them down the wrong path. Parents correcting their children at an early age may save them from a lot of heartaches in the long run. Even though it may be some children that will choose a path in life that was never meant for them to take, all because they choose to follow outside learned behaviors. But one thing is for sure, parents, if you teach them well, they will remember your teaching even if they are following outside learned behaviors. They will realize that, at some point, they can choose to listen to what they were taught or be a follower of outside learned behaviors. Some children act out of bad learned behaviors because of the way they were treated as a child. That is why when you become an adult, you must deal with so many different types of people in the workforce, church, school, and even in marriage because of their behaviors.

Not everyone was raised with two loving parents or even one loving parent or grandparent. Some were put up for adoption and removed from their homes because of mistreatment or something happened to their parents. Some children were abandoned as their parents could not take care of them because they were too young. No one knows your story, but one thing is for sure: God can rewrite your story. God can heal your hurts, pains, and wounds; this is why God's Word is so important. If you know God's word, you can help a hurting sister or brother. This is how many people turn to Christ because of what your children tell them about the word of God. Parents, all it takes is what you have taught your children in the word of God that can make all the difference. That very seed you planted in them is that very seed they will plant into the life of someone else.

I Corinthians 3:6

> I have planted, Apollos watered, but God gave the increase.

Parents, your children can do these things because of the positive behaviors they have learned. Teaching them the word of God encourages them to help others; you are never too young or too old to learn the word of God. All you must do is start where you are, even if you were not taught the word from a child, and now you are an adult, that is okay; God loves you right where you are. All you must do is pick up his word and begin reading it, join a local church, and get into a small group; God will meet you where you are. God's word will correct bad learned behaviors if the individual is willing to change. As an adult, God would place people in your life to help you grow and get to that next level in him. Every person who has given their life over to Christ has come with some type of bad learned behavior. God knows how to shape our character; you just must be willing to allow him to; not one soul came to Christ perfectly. The word of God says for all have sinned and come short of the glory of God Romans 3:23.

Giving your life to Christ will make a huge difference in your life. I am not saying that your life will be perfect, but it will get better and better the closer you get to God. God has a way of breaking, tearing down, and removing to rebuild you. When you learn to do things a certain way, and you have been doing it for a long period, it will take some work for God to reconstruct your way of doing things. And to put you on that path of doing things his way, one way to learn how God does things is through his word. Reading the word of God and doing what it says allows God to transform you from the inside out. You may not look different on the outside, but people will recognize the change on the inside. You cannot recognize a learned behavior by looking at an individual, but the way they act or react to a situation may trigger that learned behavior to come out. But when God's word gets down on the inside of the individual, their actions and reactions will be totally different from what they learned and have been doing for years. Because they thought it was the right thing to do, God's word is transforming; it can change anyone.

God wants to remove these learned behaviors, but he will take you through a process of being delivered from those learned behaviors. Sometimes, God must take the individual through a breaking process because the individual must first recognize that they have a bad learned behavior. Many times, different people will tell the individual the same thing about something that they do. They may not know that several people have told the individual the same thing, but the individual knows. Eventually, the individual may think about it and say something like, it must be me if different people are all saying the same thing. This will prompt the individual to pay close attention to this area. God wants the individual to recognize their wrongdoings before he delivers them. God would allow the individual to go through the process so they could recognize what they have been doing was wrong. Because correcting an individual for something without them knowing why you are correcting them would be a waste of time. Nothing God does is a waste of time; neither would he allow anything that the individual goes through to be a waste of time. If God delivers or corrects the individual without telling them why, then they can easily return to that wrong learned behavior. But if God takes the individual through the process of breaking this learned behavior off their life, then the individual would have learned the lesson and the consequences behind their bad learned behavior. God does not do these things to hurt the individual; He allows these things to make the individual better.

Parents, when children are corrected at an early age, these are some lessons that can be avoided in their adult lives. If learned behaviors are not corrected, the child will grow up and struggle as an adult. What your children learned growing up does not mean the entire world learned what they did. This means the world will not put up with your adult children's bad learned behaviors; it does not matter what your adult children struggle with in life. The world will not look, see, or ask for the root cause of your adult children's behavior in the workplace; the only solution they will see is a written or verbal warning that could lead to termination. The world expects your adult children to walk into their place of business having it all together like mature adults because they see the workplace as a money maker and not a therapy session. So, parents teaching and promoting bad learned behaviors may cause your children many problems in the future. These learned behaviors may be a hindrance to the individual, but if they give it to God, he will work it out. Parents, your children are here on purpose from God. When God is preparing an individual for their purpose, he will take them through the process of removing from them the things that were never intended to be there. Those learned behaviors will cause the individual problems in fulfilling their purpose for God; God will do what it takes to free the individual from these hindrance behaviors. Bad learned behaviors can cause an individual to shipwreck their life. God will allow the individual to experience certain trials and tribulations and humble them to put them on the right path in life. God wants the individual to trust Him every step of the way.

Proverbs 3:5-6

 Trust in the Lord with all thine heart and lean not unto thine own understanding. In all thy ways acknowledge him, and he shall direct thy path.

However, in doing this process, the individual may feel as if they are moving backward, but they are moving forward through the process. Because when God brings the individual out, they will come out on the other side better. In Isaiah 6:5, Isaiah said, Woe to me! I cried. I am ruined! For I am a man of unclean lips and live among a people of unclean lips, and my eyes have seen the King, the LORD Almighty.

Was Isaiah born with unclean lips? No, it was a learned behavior, but God sent an angel to pick out a burning coal and press it to Isaiah's lips. Did this learned bad behavior stop God from using Isaiah? Isaiah became one of the major prophets of God. Will God allow your adult children's learned behaviors to determine who they will become? Learned bad behaviors do not determine your adult children's destiny, nor will they determine whom God has chosen them to become. God already knew what your children were going to do even before He chose them. God gave the assignment to your children; it is already in them, and it will come forth at God's appointed time. It does not matter how messed up your children's lives may be; it does not determine the outcome of God's plans for their lives. God showed you through the prophet Isaiah that bad learned behaviors can be corrected. When an individual is saved, they can look over their life and see how they no longer do the things that they used to do. God is changing lives every day through other people. When God saves you and delivers you from those learned behaviors, do not stay saved by yourself; reach back and bring along another individual so God can do the same for them. Do not think that God cleaned the prophet Isaiah's lips just for him;

God cleaned his lips to help his people. If God did it for Isaiah, surely, he would do the same for your adult children.

Parents, even though your children may be grown adults, there may come a time when they need your advice to help them through the process of being delivered from those bad learned behaviors. Maybe a prayer or a word of encouragement because the individual will not wake up the next day and be delivered from those bad learned behaviors. It takes time; even though God can deliver the individual on the spot, it does not always work that way. God wants the individual to trust Him through the process and learn from the process so that the individual can help someone else who may be dealing with the same or similar bad learned behaviors. Not one individual grew up in a perfect home; every individual has some bad learned behaviors that they need to be delivered from, whether the individual is young or old. But the best thing about it is that all bad learned behaviors can be reversed into positive learned behaviors. It is up to the individual to want that change; the individual must want a change in life. God will never force the individual to do anything that he or she desires not to do. Change comes when the individual makes their mind up; when an individual wants something bad enough, they will do whatever it takes to get it. Change comes with discipline; to maintain change, the individual must replace it with something else. If the individual does not replace those bad learned behaviors with something positive, then the individual can easily reach back to what they once let go of.

Whenever an individual removes something negative from their life, they must replace it with something positive to avoid any setbacks. Change can sometimes be challenging; the individual may need to remove themselves from the company of certain people or stop going to certain places that would cause them to go backward instead of forward. Progress will come with a change of environment; the individual would have to place themselves in an environment and company of people who have what they are trying to achieve. Being around like-minded people would help the individual think and see things from a different perspective.

Proverbs 13:20a

He that walketh with wise men shall be wise.

The individual will become the product of their environment. If the individual is living a life that is displeasing to himself or herself, then they must change their environment and the people they keep company with. Like-minded people will think alike. The individual does not have to start with a major change; just start small by spending some time alone. Spending time alone will help the individual to evaluate themselves and to find ways to remove their bad learned behaviors and what positive behaviors they will replace them with.

For example, suppose an individual has a bad learned behavior of cursing a lot. In that case, the individual can spend more time working on their vocabulary, finding words that are more suitable for better conversations that are appropriate for their new environment.

You will attract the same type of people that you are. If an individual wants to attract different people on a different level, then they will have to do what it takes to attract the type of people that they want to be like-minded with. If the individual wants to be a lawyer, they must find a way to surround themselves with lawyers. The environment and the change of company would allow the individual to achieve positive results. It would help the individual to understand that it takes discipline and hard work to become a lawyer. However, the only way the individual would know that is if those who are lawyers tell the individual about their struggles and what it took for them to become a lawyer. The best thing about it is that the individual will have the help and support he or she needs to become a great lawyer.

Bad learned behaviors can be changed; every individual has a purpose and destiny in this life, so it does not matter how your life starts and the direction its takes. God knows how to bring individuals to a place and surround them with people who will help change their lives for the better. It is all about connecting with the right people. The path the individual must take is already lined up with those who have been chosen to help them get to their destiny. Not one individual in life should beat on himself or herself because of the hand they have been dealt; God created every individual with a purpose in mind. Perhaps the path the individual had to take was all a part of God's plan for his or her destiny. Those badly learned behaviors were a lesson for the individual to learn the difference between right from wrong and good from evil. Those lessons are for the individual to help the next person. If the individual sees another person going down that same path that they were once on, they now have the wisdom and knowledge to redirect that individual onto a better path in life. So, you can take a negative behavior and turn it into a positive behavior. It may take a little time and work, but it can be achieved. Life is all about helping the next individual to become the best that they can be. Not everyone will accept your help, but those whom God has assigned to your life will be receptive to what you have to offer. Every individual in this life has something to offer, whether they know it or just do not know it yet; every individual has a part to play in this life. It is up to the individual to be the best that they can be. So, parents continue to support and encourage your children; it does not matter how old your children are, they still need that parent talk. Just because your children are all grown up does not mean that they do not seek their parents' support.

Parents, if your children have been sheltered for most of their lives as adults, they can still fall prey to bad learned behaviors. All parents want what is best for their children; they will do anything to protect them, but do not shelter your children to the point that they do not know how to handle life without you. Life is full of lessons, and if you shelter them from life lessons, they will have a tough time trying to figure out what is right or wrong. They must be able to decipher between good and bad learned behaviors; if not, they will fall prey to the enemy, so parents, you must not allow the enemy to triumph over your children.

I Corinthians 15:33

 Do not be deceived: Bad company ruins good morals.

In every household, there are good and bad learned behaviors; there is no perfect family. In one household, you may see alcoholic parents with well-behaved children, and in the household next door, you may see what seems to be perfect parents with rebellious children. In the next household, you may see this perfect, well-put-together family, but on the inside of their household is abuse. So, how do you protect your children from unwanted learned behaviors? You can start by being positive toward them, showing them how much you love them, showering them with hugs and kisses, correcting unacceptable behavior, and praising them for acceptable behaviors. Parents, remember that your children will take the learned behaviors into adulthood, whether they are good or bad. You will hear many elderly people say it will take a village to raise a child because raising children is not easy; you will need all the help you can get. Learned behaviors can help or hurt your children; therefore, parents, it is very important that bad learned behaviors are corrected, and good learned behaviors are praised. Children want to be corrected by their parents; it shows them how much their parents care for them, and the same is true when they are praised by their parents when they do the right thing. Helping children understand life and preparing them for going out into the world and taking on life as adults is vital. The word of God teaches how to lead and guide children in life; it teaches what one can and should not do. God's word, along with prayer, will give the parent a great outcome if the child listens and takes their advice. Training and teaching children are not always easy; sometimes, it comes with hurt, disappointments, tears, and pain, but in the end, it will work out for their good.

God already knew what life would be like for each one of your children. Therefore, God chose each parent carefully because God knew what it would take to handle each child. Parents are gifted with everything they need for the children that God has placed in their care, and I do not believe that God would ever give you something that he did not think you were qualified to handle. When God gives you something, he gives it to you with the intention of knowing that you already have what it takes. Parents, when God gave you those children, you were already equipped with everything that you need to lead them. Parents, as you lead your children to becoming the best them that they can be, encourage them to build great character that possess good, learned behaviors. Good, learned behaviors can take them a long way in life, teaching them how to follow what is best for them. One must first learn how to follow before one can lead; for one to lead the right way, one must develop positive learned behaviors. Every individual is different, and they learn differently. God knows what it would take to help everyone to get on the right track. God would put people on the individual path to help them. He would also allow the individual to go through certain trials and tribulations to teach them how to trust in him. God will use certain situations or circumstances to develop the individual's character through positive learned behaviors. God would never do anything to hurt the individual, but he would do what it would take to help the individual to find their purpose in life. God wants the individual character and behavior to reflect his image.

For example, I have heard many individuals speaking to a group of people about God, and out of nowhere, they begin using obscene language, which turns the listeners away. Why? Because their character and behavior no longer reflect the image of God. Obscene language is a bad learned behavior that can be corrected, but it is up to the individual. One way the individual can develop their speaking skills is by using a different set of vocabulary.

Proverbs 4:23

 Above all else, guard your heart, for everything you do flows from it.

Luke 6:45

 For the mouth speaks what the heart is full of.

Learned behaviors can either positively help the individual or negatively affect the individual. Good, learned behaviors are always praised, but bad, learned behaviors are always looked down upon and discussed negatively. The best thing about badly learned behavior is that it can be corrected. Individuals who have developed bad learned behaviors need to surround themselves with people who have positive learned behaviors. Just because the individual has a bad learned behavior does not mean that the individual is a bad person. Every individual has some struggles, no matter who they are, but every individual has something great to offer even in the midst of their struggles. When individuals want to make a change, they must surround themselves with the type of people they want to be like so they can develop a more positive outlook on life. If you want something different, then you will have to do something different. I heard a saying, "If you keep doing the same thing, you will keep getting the same results." So, if you want different results, then change what you are doing because great minds think alike. You can also self-develop by reading positive books, listening to positive audio, and watching positive videos that demonstrate positivity because some people are visual learners. Anyone can make changes in their life if they want to, but you must put in the time and the work. You cannot attract positive outcomes with bad learned behaviors; even if the individual has a great job or owns their own business, bad learned behavior can still hinder their progress and growth. Because bad learned behaviors can run off the individual's customers and employees, positive learned behaviors can take you a long way.

God wants the best for all His children; God does not want to bless your mess. God would allow the individual to go through something that would help the individual overcome those bad learned behaviors so God can bless them in the way he wants to. There will come a time when the individual must come in touch with self, self-pride, self-arrogance, and self-ways. The individual must allow the Holy Spirit to teach him or her how to first learn to love themselves. Once the individual begins to love themselves and put God first, the Holy Spirit will step in and lead the way. It is very important that the individual loves himself or herself because many times, the individual puts everyone before him or her, and they wind up taking care of everyone and forgetting about themselves. The individual has lost touch with themselves, but the best part about this is that when the individual loves and trusts God, He will walk with the individual every step of the way until the individual realizes that he or she deserves better and is ready to raise his or her standards.

The Holy Spirit will lead the individual to people that they do not even know who will help them along their journey to becoming a better version of themselves. Whatever happened in the individual's life that caused them to develop these bad learned behaviors, whether it was past hurts, pain, disappointment, heartbreaks, or abuse. God will help the individual to overcome it all. It may not happen overnight or all at once, but if the individual puts God first and loves themselves with the love of God, he will deliver them from all those bad learned behaviors. The individual must understand that God will not let one thing that he or she has gone through go to waste. It is not what the individual has gone through but how the individual uses what they have gone through to help others become their best selves. For individuals to do that, they must start with themselves by changing the way they think and speak about themselves. Speaking positive affirmations about themselves every day is a good place to start.

The individual must not beat upon themselves when things do not change overnight because it is a process. The individual did not learn those bad behaviors overnight, and they will not change overnight, but if the individual keeps putting in the positive work by changing what he or she thinks and speaks, then they will see some progress. They must see themselves changing and tell themselves that they are changing; they must learn how to reprogram their brain. Reading the word of God is a good place to start because God's word is filled with so much encouragement. Learn the scripture and apply it throughout the day, no matter what the situation or circumstance; it will help them say the right things and do the right things. It would even help them make the right decisions. The word of God is filled with so many positive affirmations that they can speak over their lives.

For example, if life seems tough, they can speak aloud, Philippians 4:19: But my God shall supply all your need according to his riches in glory by Christ Jesus.

If they feel fearful, they can speak: II Timothy 1:7 For God hath not given us the spirit of fear; but of power, and of love, and of a sound mind.

Speaking the scripture over your situation every day is how you renew your mind and change your way of thinking. Speaking positivity over your life every day will bring positive results. If an individual keeps saying the same thing over and over, eventually, they will start to believe it. So, parents, speak positively over your children's lives so they will do the same for generations to come. Parents passing on positive learned behaviors will help their children take a better path in life.

CHAPTER 5

Pray and Watch

Parents, prayer is vital and essential for everyday living, and prayer is a necessary tool that everyone needs. Living in the world today with all the crazy things that are going on and the things that society says are right. Children nowadays are living in a world with so much peer pressure; society is telling them that it is okay to do so many things that are not right. Society is painting the wrong picture for your children, telling them it is okay to change their body parts if they are a girl, it is okay to become a boy, and if they are a boy, it is okay to become a girl. Parents, it is time to step up and take authority over these demonic spirits that are trying to claim the lives of your children; these demonic forces want to steal their identity. Parents, your children need to be covered and protected with prayers. They can become victims of gun violence in school, in neighborhoods, grocery stores, malls, movie theaters, and the list goes on and on. They are faced with so many temptations: drugs, alcohol, tobacco, social media, pornography, and hate crimes. But God is a protector, and this is why you must pray over your children and watch God work things out on their behalf.

Matthew 26:41

 Watch and pray, that ye enter not into temptation: the spirit indeed is willing, but the flesh is weak.

Parents, it is not that your children want to fall into temptations; sometimes, they do things to fit in with the crowd. Many children have the best of parents, but they still choose to make their own decisions by following others. They are dealing with so much in this world that they do not know which way to turn. They look to family and friends, but everyone is just too busy doing their own thing, and no one is paying attention to the signs that many children are crying out for help. One thing about a mother is that she can recognize change in her child; it does not matter how many children she has; she just knows when something is not right. Do not just ask the child if everything is okay; they will just tell you that everything is all right even if it is not. They do not want the parents to know what they are dealing with. Mothers: When you know that something is not right with your child, do not just ask them; stop and focus more on the child. Pay attention to the company with whom they are hanging out. Check out their emotions when they are with certain people, what type of attitude they have, and what type of character they are displaying around these individuals.

Sometimes, children are made to do things just to fit in with the crowd; it's not that the child is a bad person or that you, as parents, are not doing a good job at parenting; it can just be the type of person or people that your child has become involved with. In the world today, there is so much going on; it is like life is moving so much faster, and your children are trying so hard to keep up with the speed of life. They are not given the opportunity to be a child; at months old, they are introduced to the cell phone, and they know how to find whatever they want on your cell phone. They will even throw a temper tantrum if you take what is yours from them. They do not even know how to walk, talk, or use the potty, but they can work your cell phone. The younger children are not just talking on the cell phone, but they are using every social media platform they can log into. They are buying into all the lies that are being put out there; they do not understand that all this stuff is just a delusion. People are pretending to have what they do not really have. Parents, your children are living in a world that is moving at a rapid pace, and their little brains are trying to process it all. Your teenagers and young adult children are out there in the world trying to compete with all the lies. They are being exposed to all types of fake people through social media platforms. They think they must compete with people who are pretending to have something that they think they want or what they should have. Parents, this is why it is so important that you pray and trust God to protect and keep your children.

I Thessalonians 5:17

 Pray without ceasing.

Parents, you must pray for your children daily. You may not be on your knees twenty-four-seven, but all you must do is whisper a soft-spoken prayer to God wherever you are; God will hear your prayers. There is so much evil going on in the world that your children do not know what to believe or what not to believe. Parents, you are their role models; they are looking up to you to lead them through these dark times in life. Truth be told, they do not know what to do; they are seeking answers and directions in life. When I was much younger, I was always told that things would get worse before they got better, but it seems as if the older I get, the worse the world becomes. But I encourage myself every day by telling myself that God is still in control; He is still on the throne, no matter what it looks like. God is still the same yesterday, and today, and forever (Hebrews 13:8).

Parents, it is praying time. It is so important that you cover your children every day because things happen so quickly. But you must pray and trust God to handle the rest because he sees all and knows all; He is everywhere at the same time. He is the omnipresent God; He is omnipotent, which means he is all-powerful. He is Alpha and Omega, the first and the last, and beside Him, there is no other. That is the God I am talking about, the one who will hear your prayers and change things; that is why you must pray and trust God to do the rest.

Ephesians 3:20

> Now unto him that is able to do exceedingly abundantly above all that we ask or think, according to the power that worketh in us.

Parents, you must not allow the enemy to triumph over your children; you have the power to defeat the enemy. There is so much peer pressure out there in the world that your children are playing Russian roulette with their lives. The enemy is trying to do all that he can to destroy your children. Parents, no matter how tough it may get and no matter how deep the enemy may try to take your children, always pray God's word over your children. Why? Because God's word is truth, God is not a man that he should lie; neither the son of man, that he should repent: hath he said, and shall he not do it? Or hath he spoken, and shall he not make it good? (Numbers 23:19).

Parents, if God said it, believe that it's already done. Parents, if Satan cannot get to you, he will try to do everything in his power to get to your children. That is why it is so important that you cover your children day and night, every chance you get. Parents, you could never pray too much because many prayers are needed. Children do not tell their parents everything that they are dealing with because they do not feel as if their parents understand what they are going through. They have made decisions and choices that they feel they must live up to, even though some of their decisions and choices are bad. They are too afraid or ashamed to tell their parents what a fine mess they have gotten themselves into. They do not understand that when they have a praying mother or father who spends time with God daily, God knows them by name, and he hears their cry. They do not understand that when they are sleeping, their parents are praying, believing, and trusting God to bring them out of every bad situation, to deliver them, and to set them free from the hands of the enemy. This is why it is so important that you teach your children about God, so they will always know that they have a God who loves and cares for them no matter what is going on in their lives. They need to know that being anchored in God is a place of protection and that God loves them no matter what happens in their lives.

They need to know that God loves them with unconditional love, which means no matter how great or messy their lives may be, God will always love, cherish, and protect them for who they are. Parents, God sees your children in a different way than how you see them. Parents see their children as their babies that are dear and near to their hearts. They will do all that they can to take care of them, nourish them, teach them, love them, and the list goes on. God will love them unconditionally, teach, train, help, heal, deliver, save, stir up the gifts inside of them, chastise, break in order to rebuild, test, go through the storm with them, grow, develop, raise, meet them where they are, go through and feel their pain with them. God will give them joy, peace, and happiness; He will even be their friend. The only way they will know all these things is if they get to know him. They need to know that God is gentle, kind, caring, forgiving, patient, and loving. Children nowadays want proof; they do not just want to hear these things, but they want to see these things.

They want things to happen like a microwave instant. This is why you still need a village to raise them; the things that you tell them about God are going to be seen through the community. How you treat one another matters because they are watching. Children want to know that you see and hear them; that way, when they grow up, they do not have to seek validation from others because they will know that God has already validated them by the way they are seen, heard, and treated within the community. It takes a village to raise children, and this is why community is so important. Parents need the community to look out for them when they are not around. With the community helping and reaching out to your children, this will help your children understand boundaries. They will know what they can and cannot do in the presence of the community. In the world we are living in today, children need to know and understand boundaries; children today think that they can do whatever they please. Some children can be challenging because they think they can say whatever comes to their mind. I know this life can be rough at times, but they still need to know their place. Teaching them and studying the word of God with them, along with prayer, will teach them boundaries, and they will know their place in the community among those who really care for them.

Parents, I know life is not the way it used to be when you were growing up, but somehow, you must find your way back to the community where big momma didn't play with children. When Big Momma speaks, you shut up and listen; when Big Momma says move, you move in a hurry. When Papa gave you that look, it put so much fear in you that you were glad to get out of his sight. But big momma and Papa did not do these things to hurt or harm you; they did these things to protect you. Because big momma and papa knew what it was like in the world we live in, they even permitted others to beat you if you were caught doing something wrong, and you would beg them not to tell because you knew that would mean another beating. Parents, we all know that the world we are living in today no longer exists because nowadays children tell their parents things, and the parents want even ask questions; they just start shooting and find out later it was the wrong move, and an innocent life is taken for no reason. This is why we must go back to the community and make it a better place for all. Parents, it is so important that you continue to pray and watch God work things out. God can change any situation or circumstance; all you must do is trust and believe that he can and will. Parents, you must stop, take a deep breath, think about the world we live in today, and decide to do your part in bringing the community back together again because your children are dependent on you.

Matthew 18:20

> For where two or three are gathered together in my name, there am I in the midst of them.

Prayer is the answer to all situations. You must believe that God can handle it; God wants you to come to him and rely on him for whatever it is that you need. As children go through life, they will not always be easy because life can come with many challenges, but life challenges do not determine who they will become in life. In fact, it would help them to become better; in this life, they will learn many things. Some lessons may be tougher than others, but it is all teachable. God is the only one who truly knows their purpose for being here on earth. As a parent, you are trying your best to keep them heading in the right direction, which can sometimes be tough. Children have their minds, and sometimes, they choose to make their own decisions even if they do not take the time to consider the consequences of their decisions. Children can make decisions that may not be the worst, but they want always to be the best, either, this is why parents must always pray and watch God take the wheel and roll them in the right directions. Parents, you must pray and watch God work out the situation. You must be patient because the change in your children may not happen overnight. Sometimes, the greater the anointing, the tougher the lessons may be; anything great that was ever brought forth took a lot of work; it did not just happen overnight.

Parents, some of your children may be destined for far greater things than you can imagine, so they may have to take a different path from the others. But eventually, God will get them there. God knows just how much one can bear, so parents, do not give up on your children because God knew them even before you ever thought about them. God never makes mistakes, no matter how difficult things may seem; God wants what is best for every child. Every child is on a different path; it is a journey that only God knows where it will lead. God is the writer of every child's story; he knows the end before the beginning, and every child's story begins the moment they enter the world. Parents, you do not get to read their story before time; you only get to take the journey with them; with God, every life matters because every life was sent here on earth with a purpose from God. Some children's lives seem to be better than others, but you must keep in mind it is God who wrote their story, and every child is on a different journey to offer whatever it is that God has given to them to share with the world. So, no matter if your children's lives seem good, bad, or ugly, in every child, it is good; it is in them you must look a little harder and a little deeper because it is not always on the surface. Parents do not give up and never stop praying because God is the writer of their story. You are the perfect parents for those children. God did not give your children the choice of which family they want to be in; God chose for each of them. God's plans are far greater than one can imagine.

> Such knowledge is too wonderful for me; it is high, I cannot attain unto it.

Parents, the plans that God has for your children are so much higher than your thoughts can ever imagine for them. When God made each of them, he made them perfect for his purpose and His glory. God knew how tall he or she would be, their personality, laughter, attitude, moods, friendliness, patience, skin color, and character. He even knew the number of strands of hair that would be on their heads. God created every one of them in his image. They all have a different journey on this path called life; each of their stories will begin and end differently because they are all on a different assignment from God. Some assignments are short, and some are long, but only God gets to choose how long the assignment lasts; only God knows the length of life. Therefore, one must do all that he or she can to make the best of what God has given them. Being in this place called life, trying to find your purpose for existing through everyday living, is not always an easy journey. One must try to become their best self for the purpose that God created them to be. So, parents, as your children try to become their best selves, it is not just the beginning to the end, but it is all the in-between. Success, failures, disappointments, trials, tribulations, happiness, sadness, laughter, fun, brokenness, hurt, pain, suffering, joy, peace, love, disaster, loneliness, and so on. But this journey called life can be as beautiful as one would make it to be, but life without God, the one who created them for his purpose and glory, will never overcome all the in-between without him. This is why prayer is so key for each of their lives. Parents should encourage their children to pray as well; there can never be too much prayer because prayer can change any situation; after all, everyone needs to be encouraged.

Children need to know that they are enough, too and that they are special. They need to know that they are loved and how amazing they are. Growing up into adulthood, these things will help them throughout life, and God knows they need it. Parents, it's so important that you continue to pray for your children even as adults because this is where life can become most difficult for them. Because doing grown-up things in life can sometimes become discouraging, you must pray and watch God see them through. Even as an adult, they are still trying to become their best self. Becoming an adult does not mean that life will be challenging because it will, but one thing is for sure: God is a promise keeper. Every prayer that you have prayed over your children up until now, God has heard your cry, and the whole time, he has been working behind the scenes.

Psalm 34:15

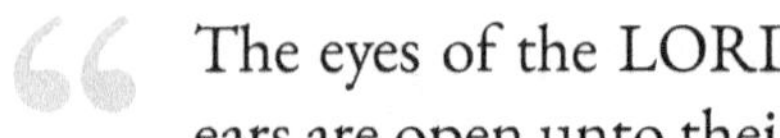

> The eyes of the LORD are upon the righteous, and his ears are open unto their cry.

God hears your cries even if it seems as if He's quiet. God hears every prayer, and He knows just when to step in. Sometimes, God must allow them to go through some things in order to keep them on the right path. I would be the first to say no one wants to go through trials and tribulations, but God will do what is necessary to help each of them get to where he is taking them in life. It may be tough, but in the end, they will be better people. God will not allow one to go through trials and tribulations to destroy them; he allows them to go through to better them. Parents, God wants them to come to him in prayer on their own; they need to know that God will answer their prayers, too. Every adult child must build a relationship with God because someday they will have a family of their own, and they will need to know how to pray for their children, also. Prayer changes things; it is times when the enemy wants you to think that God is not hearing your prayers. Because the enemy wants you to give up and throw in the towel, do not give up; keep on praying because God is working even when it doesn't seem as if he is. God may not change things right away when you ask him, but eventually, he will do so at his timing. Sometimes, God must remove some things before answering your prayers or break through those strongholds before healing some of these areas because God knows what is best for everyone.

True story: I was praying for this young lady to be saved, but the enemy would use her against me in every way possible he can use her. To be honest, sometimes I would get discouraged and not want to pray for her anymore, and one day, I went on a three-day fast for something that I was trusting God to give me an answer for. After coming off the three-day fast, I heard the young lady talking to another person, and the person asked her if she had gone to the church that I told her about, and she answered yes. She said that she liked the church and that she was going to attend that church again; the word of God says; one plant, one water, but God gives the increase 1 Corinthians 3:6. What If I had given up and stopped praying for her, parents no matter what the enemy tries to do through your children don't give up on them because prayer changes things. While you are praying, God is working on your behalf for your children; Children need to know that you care and that you are praying for them no matter how old they are; children need to know that you are concerned about what happens in their lives. Some children will act out so that you can prove your love for them; they would do anything to get your attention; children do not just act out for no reason. It is always a reason behind everything they do, even if they try to cover it up. Life can be a struggle for them, especially when they think that they must prove themselves to others. Parents, this is why they need to be covered with your prayers; you never know what they are dealing with. Parents, it may come at a time when you find out the things that your children had to go through, and it will shock you, but because of your continuous prayers, God brought them through it all.

James 5:16

> The effectual fervent prayer of a righteous man availeth much.

God will get the glory out of it all. This is why you must pray and watch God work it out. Children will always give you a reason to pray and trust God to see them through. It does not matter what path of life they are on; parents, your children still need your prayers because the enemy will try to step in and take control of their lives. Prayer will keep them covered and grounded in God's protection. It does not matter how young or old your children are; they still need the assurance of their parents' prayers. Prayer is a powerful tool that God has given, but it is powerless if you do not use it. Prayer is how we communicate with God; there is no big prayer or little prayer; you are just having a conversation with God. Some say they do not know how to pray, but that is just an excuse; God gave us a prayer in his word.

Matthew 9-13

> Our Father which art in heaven Hallowed be thy name. Thy kingdom come, thy will be done on earth, as it is in heaven. Give us this day our daily bread. And forgive us our debts, as we forgive our debtors. And lead us not into temptation but deliver us from evil: For thine is the kingdom and the power, and the glory, forever. Amen

God have given us everything that we need in His words, and

prayer is a part of that everything. Parents, when your children are struggling, pray when trouble arises in their lives. When the enemy thinks he has won them over, pray; parents, no matter what your children are faced with, all you need to do is pray and watch God see them through. Prayer is a key component for everyday living that no one should live without. There is a saying: No prayer, no power; little prayer, little power; much prayer, much power. Prayer is a powerful foundation. Parents, build your lives on this powerful foundation of prayer and watch God show out every time. Prayer builds confidence and stronger faith in God; I know there are times when the enemy wants you to doubt God because it seems as if God is not hearing you or answering your prayers. Parents, you must stand firm and know that God is working behind the scenes. God always hears your prayers, and he will answer at the right time; God designed prayer for us to be able to come to him for ourselves and wait on his timing.

Philippians 4:6

Be anxious for nothing, but in everything by prayer and supplication, with thanksgiving, let your requests be made known to God.

We know that patience is a virtue, and waiting on God to answer your prayers can sometimes become discouraging because you feel as if God is not moving fast enough. Parents, there are times when God will not move quickly for your children; sometimes, there are lessons in the process, and for them to learn the lessons, God must walk them slowly through the process to avoid their repeating the same mistakes over again. Parents, these slow processes can be painful but bearable. God will never do anything to hurt your children. God handles every situation with care; He knows what every child needs and how and when to give it to them. Some children experience trauma in life that they never discuss with anyone, but their behavior is acting out that trauma. They may be hurting on the inside and do not know what to do or how to express what they are feeling. Parents, this is why you must pray and give it to God and let him handle it; he sees all, and He knows all. God sees everything that your children are going through and what caused it. God may allow something to happen to get their attention; once God has their attention, then He can work on the core of the problem to bring complete healing to the hurt and pain in their lives. Though the scars may remain, they are just to remind them that it was God who brought them out of that hurting and painful situation. This is why you must wait on God and trust him; he knows what is best for them. So, parents never stop praying because, even as your children reach adulthood, they will still need your prayers. Parents, your prayers should never stop; you must pray for them through college, that they marry the right spouse, and that they receive Christ and stay on the right track with him. There is always a prayer to be prayed; children are not all the same, so your prayers may not be the same for every child. It is not that you love them any differently, but with some children, you must pray a little harder or maybe a lot harder; it just depends on the child and the character of their behavior.

As a parent, it does not matter how many children you have; they are all different, and there will be one child that will try you the hardest. They are the ones that you may need to pray the hardest for, but in the end, they usually are the ones who turn out to be the better children, even though you had to put in the work by praying the hardest for them. Parents just know that it is all worth it because that child did not only make you pray harder, but that child helped you to have a deeper and more intimate relationship with God. That child helped you take your prayer life to the next level. God knows what it would take to get you right where he needs you to be in your prayer life. Now, parents, you are ready to help someone else because you have put in the work, and you know what it takes to cry out until your eyes are swollen. Pray, believe, watch, and trust God to save your children and parents, and keep fighting because God has a purpose for every one of your children. Parents, to be honest, this may not come easy, nor will it happen overnight, but you must remember that God is faithful. The enemy will try to use everything in his power to fight you through your children. Why? Because Satan's job is to make you give up on your children, but God will give you the strength to press on, no matter how tough it may seem. Parents, the enemy wants to wear you out, but you must remember God has never lost a battle.

II Chronicles 20:15

 For the battle is not yours, but God's.

Exodus 14:13

 Stand still and see the salvation of the LORD.

Parents do not allow the enemy to triumph over their children. Every child has been chosen for a specific purpose, and the enemy will do all that he can to stop them from fulfilling their purpose. No one gets to choose their purpose; God does it for them. Their purpose is the reason for their being here on earth. Every child has an important role in this life, and what they carry is needed here on earth.

 But we have this treasure in earthen vessels, that the excellency of the power may be of God, and not of us.

Parents, it is your prayers, with God's protection, that keep the treasures down on the inside of them, and no matter what direction in life they may take, God is still cultivating the treasures down on the inside of them. Some children may go down a bumpy road to get to where God is taking them; parents, it is your prayer that will pull them out of those potholes and put them on that road of success where they will begin to do what God has called them to do. Walking with God is not always an easy journey, but God will see them through. Every child may not be given the purpose to become a pastor, teacher, prophet, or evangelist; their purpose may be to become a doctor, writer, caregiver, or dentist. It does not matter what direction their life is heading; God has a way of leading them to the right people who will help them on their journey. Children may not know or understand their purpose in life, so they get into trouble and feel like they have messed up so badly that they will never become who they dream of becoming. If God called you to be a judge, doctor, preacher, singer, or secretary, He knows just how to flip things upside down, and when he turns you back upside down, you will be on a journey knowing that it was nobody but God that got you there. Parents, whatever it is that your children are destined for in life, God will get them there.

Psalm 46:10

   Be still, and know that I am God:

With God, all things are possible; there is nothing too hard for God. When God is ready for an individual to walk in the things that he has chosen for him or her to do, it will happen at God's timing. God is perfect in all that He does; He knows when to say yes, no, or not yet. Parents, you must trust God in the process. Even if it seems as if the enemy is winning the battle, you must remember that God has never lost a battle. Whatever your children may be facing, it is all a part of the process. God is allowing them to go through what they are going through for a reason; you may never understand why God does things the way he does. God is the only one who knows how to bring forth the treasures on the inside of them. Many may judge your children from the outside, but the treasures lie within. There is a saying: Never judge a book by its cover. To know what the book is all about, you must open it to find out what is on the inside of it. Parents think about what is on the inside of a treasure chest; a treasure chest contains many precious jewels that are locked and placed in a secure place. Parents, your children are walking around with all those precious jewels on the inside of them, going through the process of making something great.

You see, God is the potter, and they are the clay. God knows how to mold them into whatever he created them to be. Traveling down this road called life can bring on many challenges and lessons; these are the things that make the treasures on the inside greater. A diamond cannot break if it falls onto the floor; that is why it must go through the process to sustain itself. A diamond was meant to stand out and shine like no other jewel. Parents, some of your children are diamonds, and that is why they may be facing the tougher things in life; they were created to stand out from all the rest. When God finishes with that diamond, it can stand the storms of life. When the storm is over, that diamond will shine so beautifully because a true diamond carries a great investment and brings in a great profit that will glorify its owner. God knows how to bring out the best in them. Parents, this is why it is so important for you to pray for your children; you do not know what they are carrying. Every human being came to earth with their purpose on the inside of them; the greater the purpose, the more the enemy will fight to keep their purpose from being fulfilled; praying for your children on a daily basic helps them to overcome the fiery darts of the enemy.

Isaiah 54:17

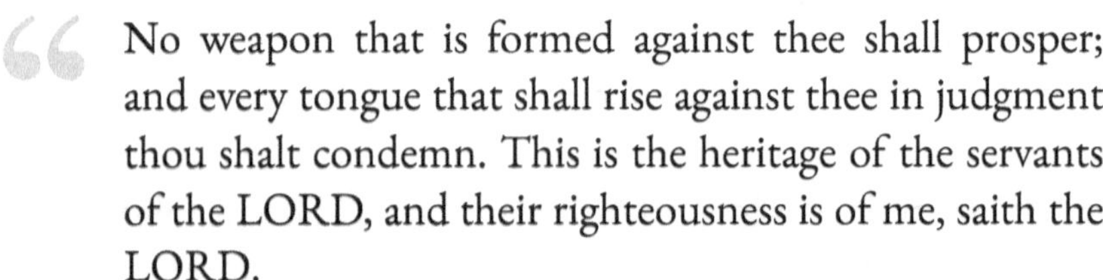

> No weapon that is formed against thee shall prosper; and every tongue that shall rise against thee in judgment thou shalt condemn. This is the heritage of the servants of the LORD, and their righteousness is of me, saith the LORD.

So, parents keep on praying and watch God work it out. God knows just when to turn things around; God's timing is not on your watch, but at his perfect timing, it will all come together.

CHAPTER 6

Victory for the overcomers

Parents, after every war, there will be victory. While you are on your knees doing warfare prayers, God is fighting the battle for you and your children. When the enemy thought he was having victory over your children, your prayers helped them get up and get back in the race. Parents, it was your prayers that encouraged them not to throw in the towel; it was your faith that knew that the victory was already won; whenever God's children walk according to his will and keep his commandments, they will always overcome and have the victory over the enemy.

Romans 8:31

If God is for us, who can be against us?

Parents do not look at the situation that your children are going through and see defeat; look at the situation and see victory. Never speak negativity over your children; always speak positivity over them, no matter how messed up their lives may be.

Isaiah 59:1

 Behold, the LORD's hand is not shortened, that it cannot save.

Parents, let not the enemy triumph over your children; there were times when you had to fast and pray for your children's deliverance, and now you are seeing the fruit of your labor. I know there have been times when you cried out all night long, walking the floor, praying, and believing that God would turn their lives around. Though you may have lost some sleep, it was all worth the lives of your children being saved; God never said that this life would be easy, but he promised that he would see you through. Though the storms of life may rage, and the winds may blow, one thing is for sure: the storm will not always last; there is always a light at the end of the tunnel; after all the praying now, you can finally see some victories. Because at the end of the storm, there is always victory for the overcomers. Parents never stop praying for your children because there are always more victories to be won; there is nothing like looking back and seeing the fruit of your labor and how far God has brought your children. Parents, speaking with your children and hearing some of the stories from your children about the life they were living, then you know why God had you up all night praying them through.

You must know that God is bigger than any battle; He knows when enough is enough. All you must do is have faith, trust, and believe that God is always there through the good times and the tough times. Whenever you and your children are going through something, God is going through it with you all, and when you and your children are smiling, just know that God is smiling too. God made a promise that he will never leave you nor forsake you (Hebrews 13:5). When God's children obey him, there is no good thing that he will withhold from them that walk uprightly (Psalm 84:11). Therefore, you know that the victory is already won; it does not matter what your children must face in life it will only make them stronger because it is all a part of the process for where God is taking them. There are many things in life that your children must go through for them to know that God will bring them out. Parents and your children need to know that they need God. Those who are perfect does not need a savior, but those who are imperfect need a savior to show them that God will give them victory if they trust Him. Parents, God wants your children to come to him with all their imperfections; your children's imperfections give God the opportunity to show others that with him, all things are possible. Because all the victory belongs to Jesus, and if the victory belongs to Jesus, then it belongs to his children, too.

Romans 8:17

> And if children, then heirs; heirs of God, and joint heirs with Christ; if so be that we suffer with him, that we may be also glorified together.

Parents, this means that your children will overcome and share the same victories with Jesus Christ. After praying all night, walking the floor, and trusting God, there can be nothing but victories for you and your children. Parents' prayers work in every situation and circumstance. One thing about children is that they will keep you praying, and God is always there with a listening ear because he has the answer to every situation and circumstance, knowing that you are an overcomer and that the victory is already won. Children come in all sizes and ages, and there is no such thing as one being too young or too old to receive the prayers of their parents. One thing about parents is that they will never stop praying for their children no matter how old they become; this is the type of love parents have for their children.

 But thanks be to God which giveth us the victory through our Lord Jesus Christ.

God takes care of his children, and he will forever give them the victory over the enemy. Parents, all you need to do is keep on praying, trusting, and believing, knowing that the victory is already yours in Jesus' name. Prayer is a battleground where victories are won, so parents, stay on your battleground for your children because the enemy will try to do all that he can to break you so he can destroy your children. Parents let not the enemy triumph over your children. Children are human beings; they are not perfect, and parents cannot put them in a bubble trying to protect them. Your children will go through life lessons to become who God has chosen them to be. This is why you must continue to pray for their victories. There will be many obstacles, but God will bless them to be overcomers, and he will give them victory over every obstacle. Even when it looks like they are losing the battle, just remember they are winning because God has never lost a battle. Parents, no matter what they are faced with in this life, know that God has it all under control. God will not allow anything to happen to your children that was not already predestined to happen; remember, nothing takes God by surprise. Children are chosen for God's purpose and His will. Truth be told, God is in control of every area of their lives. God knows what they are going to do even before they do it; God knows all things. Children go through life trying to figure out who they are. As parents, sometimes you try to figure it out for them, and you try to keep them on the right path in life, but it does not always work the way you planned for it to work. Because God knows more about their path and journey in this life than any parent can ever figure out, so keep the faith, keep trusting God and know that God will see them through because with God, there is always victory on the other side of through.

Parents, no matter what storms your children may face, just know that storms do not always last; there is always a rainbow to remind you that you are an overcomer, and the victory belongs to you and your children when the storms are over. When your children walk in obedience to you, they are walking in obedience unto God, and obedience always brings victories.

Colossians 3:20

> Children obey your parents in all things: for this is well pleasing unto the Lord.

Parents and children are not perfect; they have their minds, and there are times when they will use their judgments and make decisions that you may disagree with. But it is all about growth and learning how to make the right decision apart from their parents. Children cannot go through life being micromanaged by their parents, and you cannot keep them in a glass house; you must allow them to become their own person. The person that God has chosen them to become they want always to make the right choices or decisions, but that does not mean that God will not give them victory. Sometimes, life can be difficult and complicated; this is why you must continue to pray for your children's victories. Praying for your children daily will bring daily victories. Parents, your prayers are what keep the enemy from triumphing over your children.

 The thief cometh not, but for to steal, and to kill, and to destroy I come that they might have life, and that they might have it more abundantly.

With God, it does not matter how a situation may look; just remember that God has all victories in His hands. God has the first, the in-between, and the last say. Parents, the enemy's job is to distract your children from becoming whom God has chosen them to become; the enemy wants to stop them from reaching their full potential in the things that God has already invested in them. Children go on with their everyday lives, not focusing on what the enemy is trying to do in their lives. They want to hang out with their friends, go to the mall, or to a party, the enemy is not on their mind, and the enemy knows this. This is how the enemy tries to trap them to take them down roads they were never intended to take. Parents, your children just want to live their lives pure and innocent, not knowing that the enemy is plotting against their lives every day on how he can destroy them. Parents, your children are not aware of Satan and his tactics if they have not been taught about these things; Satan is a trickster trying to allure your children away from you through disobedience and rebelliousness so he can destroy them.

> For we wrestle not against flesh and blood, but against principalities, against powers, against the rulers of the darkness of this world, against spiritual wickedness in high places.

Parents, because of your prayers and faithfulness in God, he will protect your children from the hands of the enemy. God will see for your children when they cannot see for themselves. Trust and believe in God, knowing that he will bring your children out of Satan's evil tricks and schemes. It is so important that you teach your children about God and study his word with them, so they are aware of Satan and all his lies. Taking them to church is a great start because they will get the opportunity to learn about God with their peers on their level. They can also hear the testimonies of their peers on how God delivered and brought them out of the traps and schemes of Satan. This can alert them to know that they are not exempt from the schemes and tactics of Satan, and maybe it will help them make better decisions. Sometimes, as parents, it is hard to reach your children and get them to understand these things, but for whatever reason, they tend to listen to their peers, whether they are in the church or outside the church. However, being in the church, there are other adult Christians that your children can turn to who are willing to listen to them and help them overcome these dilemmas in life. Some children will keep these crises in their lives to themselves, which is not healthy for them; it can cause anxiety and depression, which can also lead to suicidal thoughts. Children deal with things differently, and some can cope with the dilemmas in their lives by talking to their parents because they feel comfortable doing so.

On the other hand, there are those children who do not have that same comfort level when talking to their parents about anything that is going on in their lives. In this life, children need someone they can trust with the things that they are dealing with. Someone who will not spread rumors about what they discussed with them or judge them, but someone willing to help them overcome the tricks and schemes of the devil.

I John 4:4

 Little children, you are from God and have overcome them, for he who is in you is greater than he who is in the world.

Parents, God loves your children, and he will do whatever it takes or use whomever it takes to stir your children in the right direction, but he will not allow the enemy to triumph over them. God will always bring them out with victory, and they will overcome the tricks and schemes of the devil. Parents, your children need to know that there is a champion who lives on the inside of them, and he is called the Holy Spirit, the one who can teach them all things and bring all things back to their remembrance. He will never leave them alone. God will always give victory to the overcomers. Children go through a lot of things that their parents don't even know about because they never share them with their parents; they think that their parents are too old to understand what they are going through and not know that all the restless nights walking the floors and praying at all hours of the night are what helped them become overcomers and gain victory over the enemy. Parent your children; they do not have life figured out, but each day, they struggle to find their place in this world. Parents, teaching your children at a young age how to trust God and have faith in him would be a whole lot better for them. When God tells them to walk away from some of the things in life, they will be able to walk away with no fear. They will know how to let go when the time comes, with faith in God, knowing that he has their back. Parents, God wants your children to trust Him wholeheartedly, knowing that he will see them through every situation and circumstance.

Parents, God has a plan for your children's lives, and the devil does not want to see it come to pass, but God will give them the victory to overcome the enemy. Children depend on their parents a lot because they do not know that God is the one who provides for them through their parents. They do not know God as their deliverer, healer, or way maker because they must be taught that God is the one who works out every situation in their lives; God is the one who blesses them to overcome the enemy through victory. It may be their parents who are praying, but it is God who is answering the prayers. Children need to be taught the truth about who God really is. They need to know that everyone needs to depend on God to give them the victory to overcome the things of the world. Children can learn anything that the world has to offer; surely, they can learn the things that God has to offer. Parents, if you teach your children the word of God, then they will learn the word of God. If you teach them to trust and have faith in God, then they will trust and have faith in God. If you teach them that God will give them the victory to overcome the things of the world, then they will believe that God will give them the victory to overcome the things of the world. Parents, you can help to mold the minds of your children because children believe whatever their parents tell them. Parents, you are your children's first teachers, and you are the ones molding their minds for the outside world. And whatever you teach them during this time in their lives will stick with them.

 Do not be conformed to this world but be transformed by the renewal of your mind, that by testing you may discern what is the will of God, what is good and acceptable and perfect.

Parents, your renewed minds will help to better mold and develop the minds of your children, teaching them that whatever comes their way, God has the power to bring them out with victory as overcomers from the things of the enemy. Parents, every decision and thought starts in the mind; this is why the enemy goes for the mind. The enemy, Satan, wants to control the mind; that is why it is so important to read, study, and meditate on the word of God. The word of God is transforming, and it will renew the mind, change your way of thinking, and change the way you see and do things. The word of God will change you from the inside out.

Philippians 2:5

 Let this mind be in you, which was also in Christ Jesus.

Parents, whatever you feed your children's minds and whomever you allow to feed their minds will become their mindset. Life comes with choices, and those choices come with consequences. If the choices are good, then you know that the consequences will be great, but if the choices are bad, then you know that the consequences will not be a good outcome. Parents, teaching your children the word of God daily will help them immensely. If you study one scripture per week, you take that one scripture and learn it, discuss it, apply it, believe it, act on it, and have faith in it. Parents, this will help your children in ways you will never imagine. I stress this because many believers read, quote, and pray the scripture, but they do not believe or have the faith to believe that what it says will happen. Teaching your children the importance of having faith and believing what the word says will help them as overcomers to know that the victory is theirs even before it happens why because the word of God says so.

Hebrews 11:1

> Now faith is the substance of things hoped for, the evidence of things not seen.

Parents, it says, now faith is the substance of things hoped for. Substance is what God's word says will happen, and you have faith to believe in His word. The substance is there, but it is like it is in a secret place waiting to manifest what you are believing for. You know the evidence is not seen, but you, through faith, believe it will appear to you in the physical manifestation. Parents, do not look at where your children are in life now but see them where you are, believing God to take them in Him. Parents, for God to take your children where he wants them to be in him, you must learn to let go and let God have his way in their lives. Parents do not stand in the way when God is teaching your children; allow God to have his way in their lives because God knows what is best for them. When God is chastising your children, stop trying to accept the consequences for them because this will not help them; it will only delay the process. Allow them to go through it with God. This is how God builds their faith and teaches them how to believe and trust in him because God is the only one who knows the purpose and plans that he has for their lives.

Through God, they will always be overcomers and win the victory because the battle is not theirs. It is the Lord's. Parents choose to do things God's way. There is no way you can go wrong as parents. God will give you clear directions and instructions on how to handle your children. You know all children are different, which means the directions and instructions will be different for each child. You may need to be harder on one child than the other, and it is not because you loved one more than the other. They may say something like this, "Mom and Dad love this one or that one more." But this is how the enemy wants them to see it, now they do not recognize that the harder things are, or the tougher things are. It is because God has chosen them for something greater, and the devil uses all these distractions to throw them off course and to take their minds off where God is taking them in life. Satan wants them to lose focus on life, and the only way they can find their way back to their rightful place is in God.

Parents, if your children follow the leadings of God, then they will understand why the directions and instructions from God through their parents were necessary. When they begin to see how their lives are flourishing and how God is using them to help him transform the lives of others, then they will begin to see the big picture as to why life growing up for them was hard. Then, they will realize that nothing great comes easily and greatness is always born through pain. The greater the pain, the greater the call, and the greater the blessings in their lives. Parents let God have his way in your children's lives and allow him to birth something great through them. Parents, you cannot change your children, and neither can you fix their lives. Only God can do that. You must allow them to experience God on their own so they can learn who God is for themselves. If you keep helping them with every step they make in life, then they will forever depend on you and not on God, and they will believe that they are overcomers and win the victory because of what you have done for them and not what God has done for them.

Parents think about the time when your children were toddlers, and they were learning how to walk, and you had faith to believe that you could let go and they would walk on their own. Well, parents, you must have that same faith and belief to let their hand go and allow them to walk with God, not to say that they will not need you because they will. You just need to know when God is allowing you to step in and help them. Parents raising children can be a challenge because when you think that you have it all figured out, God will shift things in a different direction that would make you second guess yourselves. Why? Because even as parents, God must remind you that he is the one in control. Parents, you do not have to plan your children's future. God has already done that. All you need to do is support them in getting there because you can only take your children so far in life. But God can take them to places in life that they would never imagine being there; God's plans are far greater for their lives than you know, so parents, when your children come to those bumps in the road, just know that God has it all under control. God will bless them with victory because they are overcomers in Christ Jesus. Parents, there is no child exempted from the trials of life; therefore, you should always keep your children in prayer before God.

Because God is everywhere, he sees all things, and he knows all things, God can get your children to do things, and they will not understand why they are doing it. Parents, when you pray for your children, and they run into bumps in the road or their lives are in danger, God will lead them to safety. Parent's prayer is a powerful tool that can be used anywhere at any time. Parents, God will not allow the enemy to triumph over your children. He will always give them victory because they are overcomers' parents. God hears your prayers. God wants you to trust him through the process with your children; God will take care of you and your children. He will never allow the enemy to overtake you or your children.

 For the LORD, your God is the one who goes with you to fight for you against your enemies to give you the victory.

God is the one who is in control of all things. Parents, when God fights for you and your children, just know that the enemy has already been defeated, and you are overcomers with the victory. Parents do not forget that your children are human spirit beings; therefore, the battle is spiritual, and this is why spiritual warfare prayers are needed because life is spiritual in every aspect. Parents let not the enemy steal the souls of your children because your prayers are a weapon. So, do not allow the enemy to triumph over your children. No matter how tough it may get, just remember God has never lost a battle. Therefore, you have already won the victory because you are overcomers in Christ Jesus.

CHAPTER 7

Equipping Your Children for The Future

Parents know that you have equipped your children with all that God has prepared them with to help them on this journey called life. Teaching your children God's ways for life according to his word, God's word can lead and guide them on this path for the future.

Psalm 119:105

 Thy word is a lamp unto my feet and a light unto my path.

Parents, you may not know where the future will take your children, but if you trust God, he will direct their feet every step of the way. Making God a part of your children's lives is the best gift you could ever give them. Parents, the world has taught things like You must go to college to have a bright future. Parents, your children's future is in God's hands. There is nothing wrong with going to college, but when you take that secular education and combine it with God's teaching, you will have a much greater outcome. Parents, God is the one that holds your children's future, so equipping your children with both can take them to many places in God. God knows how to take that secular knowledge and use it to their advantage; God knows how to use it to glorify him in all that your children do. Parents equipping your children with the principles of God's word will take them a long way. God has already set everything up from the beginning to the end; all your children must do is follow his lead and allow him to navigate them on this journey called life. God knows the future that he has for each of your children. Even though all their futures look different, God is still the navigator.

Jeremiah 29:11

> For I know the plans I have for you, declares the LORD, plans to prosper you and not to harm you, plans to give you hope and a future.

You see, parents, God planned your children's future even before you ever thought of having them. God is their future planner; He knows just what he has planned for their lives. One thing about God's plans is that you never know how they will turn out. God will allow your children to mess up so badly in life that you almost want to give up on them. But with God, it is all a part of His plan; parents' life lessons will also prepare them for the future. Sometimes, God will let them go out into the middle of the ocean before they realize that they are drowning and need God's help. Parents do not fret because God knows how to get your children's attention. Remember, God is the God of your children's future. Parent, the future is not what you think it is, but the only way you will know what the future means is to seek God, and he will make it known unto you through his word, parents. To know and seek God is to know his mystery.

 And he said unto them, unto you it is given to know the mystery of the kingdom of God.

Parents, everything that your children need is already within them because God knew their future even before their lives began. God knows what he equipped them with because he has plans for the treasures on the inside of them. Every gift on the inside of your children is to be used for the glory of God, regardless of what that gift may be, whether it is a doctor or a preacher. The gift is to glorify God and God only. Parents, it is very important that you do the best you can to equip your children's future for the kingdom of God by teaching them to study the word of God and pray his word. Because the devil will do all that he can to trick your children out of their gifts to glorify him and not God. The devil will offer them worldly riches, fame, and all the things that this world has to offer in the pleasing of the natural eyesight. The devil wants to be like God, so he would try to steal your children's future for his kingdom because the devil is jealous of the love that God has for his children. A good father wants what is best for his children, and he knows this, so parents' cover your children in prayer and pray that God will protect his treasure on the inside of them. For some children, God will use these treasures at an early age, and for some at a more mature age, it depends on whatever God has placed on the inside of them. Parents, you do not know where the future will take your children.

Ecclesiastes 8:7

> For he knoweth not that which shall be: for who can tell him when it shall be?

Only God knows what the future holds, so parents who know how to better equip your children for the future than the one who created them. God is the creator of all things, including humankind. God has not created anything just to create it. God created all things with a purpose and plan in mind. The most important thing is waiting on God. Parents, you cannot force God's plans for your children because their future is in the hands of God and not yours. God's plans are perfect in every way, so parents, you must remember that it was God who sent forth your children in the beginning. They were born at the right time and created in his image for his plans for their lives. God knows exactly what he is doing. God will protect your children's future because many depend on the blessings that your children's lives have to offer. Parents, what God has invested in your children, others future is depending on what God has to offer them through your children. God works through those who will allow his will to be done through them, parents. This is why you must keep your children in prayer and encourage them to pray and read the word of God. No one knows what the future holds.

Isaiah 55:8

> For my thoughts are not your thoughts, neither are your ways my ways saith the LORD.

Parents, you cannot figure out your children's future because you do not know the plans or thoughts of God. God has been leading your children from birth because he is the only one who knows what your children were created to bring forth in this life. Doing life with God

You may think you know his next move, and he moves in a totally different direction on you. This is why it is so important to let go and allow him to do the work through your children. Parents, when you allow God to have His way, your children's future will shine even brighter. Parents, you do your part and allow God to do his part, helping your children to pray, read the Word, control their attitude, and be mindful of their behavior. Teaching them that character is important, respecting others, and knowing how to submit to authority in its proper perspective is essential. Parents your children are the future, and the way you equip them for it can make the world a better place or not a better place. It depends on the work you put into equipping and teaching them how valuable they are. Children need to know that they matter. Their opinions, ideas, choices, and decisions matter. Parents equipping your children for the future in God can make life so much easier with fewer heartaches. Parents, you can only do the best that you can and leave the rest to God.

God knows how to make up for all the shortcomings; God is the center of your children's lives. Leaving God out of the preparation will leave a huge void in your children's lives. Trying to do life without the One who created them for his purpose can easily become a shipwreck for them. Parents, without the guidance of the Holy Spirit, bad choices and decisions can be made, and wrong directions can be taken, which all can happen if one is not careful. Choosing to follow the leading and guidance of the holy spirit can lead to godly success. Godly success is when you fulfill your God-given purpose in life, which God chose you to fulfill. Whatever God created you to fulfill here on earth is your God-given purpose.

Life lessons teach one how to prepare for the future; your struggles and shortcomings cause you to turn to God for help because some feel as if they can do it all on their own. But to fulfill your God-given purpose, you will need God to fulfill his purpose through you. So, parents, every road your children take in life can be a part of their preparation for their future. Life can be so complicated, but God knows how to bring it all together to work out for their good. Parents helping to prepare your children for the future will not always be easy; there will be some hiccups, bumps in the road, and disappointments, but most of all, there will be many wins. So, hang in there because you never know what the future holds for your children. Parents, this is why it is so important to keep your children lifted in prayer and teach them the word of God.

Deuteronomy 11:18-19

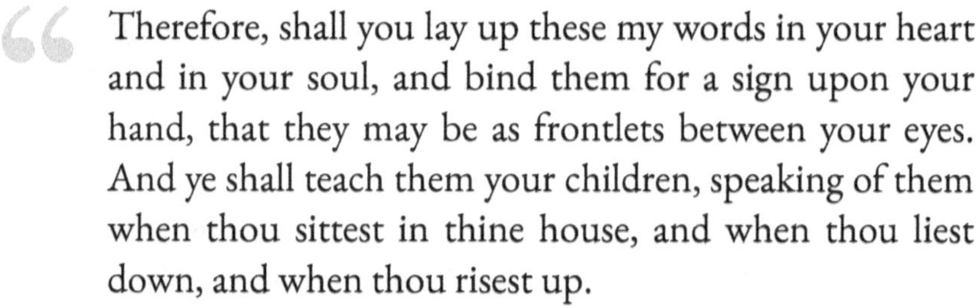

> Therefore, shall you lay up these my words in your heart and in your soul, and bind them for a sign upon your hand, that they may be as frontlets between your eyes. And ye shall teach them your children, speaking of them when thou sittest in thine house, and when thou liest down, and when thou risest up.

Parents, you teach your children, and they teach their children. It should continue to be taught generations after generations, so parents, it is important to incorporate the word of God into your children's future because it was meant to be a part of their lives. Parents allow your children to step into their future, knowing who they are and who they are. As a parent you can only take your children so far but by equipping them with God, their future will be so much brighter. Parents' preparation means a lot because when you are equipped and prepared for something, it makes a world of difference. Parents, your children will know what they are doing and understand what they are doing in life because you took the time to equip them for the future. Parents, for your children to fulfill their God given purpose it is so important that they are equipped for their future endeavors. Even though God has already equipped them with everything that they need, parents, whether your children are called or chosen by God, still need to be equipped for the future because the enemy would try to bury the very thing that God has called and chosen your children to do.

Hebrews 13:20-21

> Now may the God of peace, who through the blood of the eternal covenant brought back from the dead our Lord Jesus, that great shepherd of the sheep, equip you with everything good for doing his will, and may he work in us what is pleasing to Him, through Jesus Christ, to whom be glory forever and ever. Amen.

Parents, God already knows what he has called or chosen each child to do here on earth, but sometimes life can become so chaotic that they can lose sight of what life is really all about. Choosing to live life God's way and not their way can be life-changing for them. Parents, sometimes life does not always go in the direction you plan for your children. Parents doing things God's way does not always come easy, but it comes with the best outcome. God knows what is best for every child, even if you, as parents, disagree with some of the outcomes for your children. God would not let one thing that your children had to endure go to waste; God would use everything that they had to endure for his glory. So, no matter what your children must face in life, God has a purpose for it all. Equipping them can help them to reflect on their future, and it would allow them to stay on the right path.

Parents, when you equip your children for the future, it helps them to see life differently. No one knows their true purpose in life without knowing, being directed, and connected to God. God is the one who would guide your children to the purpose that he has chosen for them to fulfill here on earth. In this life, every child matters regardless of their race, color, or nationality; parents, your children chose neither one of these; God did the choosing for them. All children have a purpose, and wherever God places them and to whomever parents they are entrusted, it is all a part of God's plans. Parents equipping their children for the future can also teach them how to handle the dos and don'ts in life. It can help them to identify what to accept and what not to accept. It would teach them how to walk away from toxic people and situations, this is why it is so important that your teaching comes from the word of God.

John 15:5

> I am the vine. Ye are the branches: He that abideth in me, and I in him, the same bringeth forth much fruit: for without me ye can do nothing.

Parents, this is why it is so important that your children are connected with God; apart from him, they can do nothing. Parents, you may not know your children's future, but it is important that you know the One who knows your children's future. God is the source of all that you need; God's Word is filled with all the promises that he promised for His people. All you must do is walk according to his will. Parents, I know that the world would tell you that children do not come with instructions, but that's not true because God's word is filled with instructions on how to raise your children. It is filled with wisdom, knowledge, and understanding of how to do things God's way. So, by teaching and equipping your children for the future according to God's word, you cannot go wrong. God's promises are yes and amen. Parents, if you lead your children down the right path in life and you have taken them as far as you can, God will step in and do the rest; after all, He is the one who knows your children's future. Parents, no matter what path in life your children may go down on their own, just know that your labor is not in vain.

II Corinthians 4:7

> But we have these treasures in earthen vessels, that the excellency of the power may be of God, and not of us.

Parents, it is not about you or your children; it is about God using the gifts that he has placed down on the inside of your children.

I Corinthians 6:19-20

> Know ye not that your body is the temple of the Holy Ghost, which is in you, which ye have of God, and ye are not your own? For ye are bought with a price: therefore, glorify God in your body and in your spirit, which are God's.

Parent's God idea for your children's future may look totally different from what you see that your children's future can become. You know that they have great potential, parents. You see it as potential, but God sees it as an opportunity for his will to be done. Parents, have you ever wondered how your children arrived at the place where they are in life? Maybe you had to ask God how your children got there. You may have one child in college, one dropped out of school, one working, one on drugs, one pregnant, and another very successful in life. Even though all the children have the same parents, they all have different futures, and no matter if one life looks worse than the other, that does not determine their worth. God's greatest blessing can come through the school dropout, the one on drugs or the pregnant mom, and not to discredit that child in college is the successful one in life. God does not have respect of person. God has a purpose for them all, so parents do not allow the devil to cause you to reject your children because their lives do not measure up to your standards.

Parents, continue to pray for all your children, no matter where they are in life. Just keep in mind that their future is in God's hands. Parents' everyday lives can be a life lesson; these lessons can also equip your children for their future. Life can be a challenge at times, but if you trust God, he will see you through, and know that this, too, shall pass. Equipping your children for the future can bring on some emotional and stressful situations at times but remember that nothing that you or your children go through. God will not allow it to go to waste; God has a purpose for it all. Parents, no matter how hard you may try to be, even on your best days, the enemy will try to bring distractions and chaos into your family.

Because your children do not understand that the battle is in the mind, the enemy will try to use anything and anybody to get into the minds of your children to paint a picture that you are the enemy in their lives. Especially if you are praying parents, the enemy's goal is to try and destroy you through your children because the enemy knows that you will keep your children covered in prayer. Parents, your children have no idea of the gifts that they are carrying around on the inside of them, so the enemy will try everything in its power to stop those gifts from coming to fruition. The enemy would use drugs, rebelliousness, disobedience, teen pregnancy, other people, alcohol, distractions, and so many other things to throw your children off track. Parents do not give up; keep on praying your children through.

Isaiah 54:17

> No weapon that is formed against thee shall prosper; and every tongue that shall rise against thee in judgment thou shalt condemn. This is the heritage of the servants of the LORD, and their righteousness is of me, saith the LORD.

Romans 8:31

> What shall we say to these things? If God be for us, who can be against us?

Parents, that very thing that the enemy tried to use to destroy your children will become one of their greatest testimonies. The harder the enemy fights your children, the greater the gifts they are carrying, so parents do not give up because this is all a part of equipping your children for the future. One day, your children will realize Satan and his evil schemes, and though they may not appreciate you now, one day, they will. Being a parent comes with a lot of responsibility because you are trying to get your children to understand the things that they are not interested in hearing. As parents, you have been down many roads in life, and you try to teach your children to avoid some of those unpleasant roads that you had to learn lessons. Parents, if you had not taken those roads, you would not have learned the lessons that came along with them. Therefore, there will come a time when you must allow them to go down some of those unpleasant roads so they can learn the lessons that are necessary for their future. I know, as parents, you would like to make everything easy for your children but think about your relationship as children of God. God does not make everything easy for His children; He allows his children to go through many things not to harm them but to use them to strengthen and grow them. God uses these things to prepare his children for their future because he knows where he is taking them in life.

As parents, sometimes you go through things, and it feels like that thing is going to take you out. When you see your children going through it, you want to do all that you can to prevent them from experiencing it. But you must remember that it is necessary to prepare them for their future; parents, some of the greatest things are born through pain. God knows how much your children can bear. Parents, it is funny how life works: as young children, your children are being prepared for life.

For example, a young girl is prepared to be a wife, home keeper, and mother. She's given a doll to care for, a doll house that comes with a kitchen, bathroom, living room, and a bedroom filled with furnisher, cooking utensils, and a male doll as a mate for her doll. These things are to prepare her for the future. On the other hand, your young sons were always given a car, truck, train, or an airplane, so when they grew up, these are the things that they cherished most because this is what was given to prepare them for their future, so when you see them outside as a man shinning up their new car, or truck done judge them because they were prepared for this.

Isn't it funny that people would say something like this: Girls are more mature than boys, and they grow up faster than boys, so parents, how you prepare your children for the future is very important, even at a young age. If you teach your children the ways of God, it will not depart from them; even if they stray away, God has a way of bringing them back to him. This life is preparation for what God has chosen to do through one's life; God has a purpose for every human being born here on earth. So, parents, no matter what direction your life has taken your children, it was all to prepare them for the future. Parents do not beat upon yourselves because you do not feel as if you have gotten it right; just remember it will all come together and work out for their good. Parents, pat yourselves on the back because you did the best that you could do to equip your children for the future. God's blessings be with you.

Proverbs 24:14

 You have a positive outcome ahead of you. The future is bright, and the best is yet to come.

CHAPTER 8

New Beginnings

Parents, now it is time for new beginnings. New beginnings give you the opportunity to do things differently, so regardless of your past mistakes, it is time for you to put those things behind you and step into your new beginnings.

Philippians 3:13

> But this one thing I do, forgetting those things which are behind and reaching forth unto those things which are before.

Parents: you cannot change what happened in the past, so it is time to release yourselves from the past and step into new beginnings. Just because you are a parent does not mean that you are perfect. One thing that you can do is start by acknowledging God in your new beginnings by asking him to lead you down the path that he will have you take with your children. Because with God, it is never too late to start over again. God is a God of many chances; He wants you and your children to win in this life. God wants what is best for your children. Parents, helping your children by focusing on God and his perspective of life, seeking him for what it is that he wants, and choosing to do things God's way will give you and your children a better way of seeing life.

Parents, you can begin a new by listening more to what your children have to say, and vice versa; the children need to listen more to what their parents are saying, and everyone needs to listen more to what God has to say. Parents, in your new beginnings, there is no way you can do life without God because life without God is void and without purpose. Have you ever heard the saying that if you want something different, then you must do something different if you want a different outcome? Parents, perhaps you did not get it right the first time, but God will always give you new beginnings to get it right the next time. That is just how amazing he is. One thing about God is that he never gives up on his children. Parents as you step into your new beginnings with your children, picture the change that you want to see, and once you see it, then believe that it will come to fruition. Remember, parents, nothing happens overnight; it is a process to get there because children see things on a totally different level than parents do. Children look at life as being in the present and not as being in the future because they believe that they already have life all figured out. They do not know that life comes with many obstacles, trials, tribulations, ups and downs, and many decisions that need to be made. But parents, it is okay because God got this in this new season of your new beginnings.

Matthew 9:17

 Neither do people pour new wine into old wineskins. If they do, the skins will burst; the wine will run out and the wineskins will be ruined. No, they pour new wine into new wineskins, and both are preserved.

Therefore, parents, you are no longer operating in your old ways; you are now operating in a new way. God has given you new opportunities to walk in your new beginnings. Parents, sometimes it will take you walking along in your new beginnings with God long before your children will come alongside you, but God knows what he is doing when it comes to your children. God knows just how much work it will take to get them there. New beginnings are always great because they give you the opportunity to rethink the way you do and respond to certain situations. They also give you the opportunity to deal with your children differently because whenever you are in doubt, you can always seek God to help you make the right decision. Parents, as you step into your new beginnings, your children, as well as others, will see your change, and believe me, children notice many things, especially when it comes to their parents.

My children tell me that we are not living in the times when you were born; things are totally different, and I tell you that I totally agree with them. Because when I was growing up, we did not have access to any of the things that they have access to now. The fact there were no cell phones, and if it were, my parents could not afford to buy one for me and my sibling because there were too many of us. Coming from a large family, we were each other's entertainment, and that is right, we had to entertain each other. So, parents, the time we are living in now is totally different because things change with time, and nothing remains the same. You may not have ever faced the things that your children must face at their age. This is not to say that parents have never faced anything. It is just that they faced life in a different era. So, parents, this gives you the opportunity to sit back and reassess things and how you can do things differently.

Children expect their parents to have an answer for every situation and circumstance that happens in life. Children nowadays see and go through a lot, and even though you grew up in a different era, they still expect you to know what is going on in their era. Parents, life is changing every day, and your children are faced with a whole lot more challenges. Growing up in this era is so much tougher than some of your children can handle. This is why it is so important that you and your children have a relationship with God: because God will see you through all the bumpy roads in life. Parents, hang in there and know that God is with you every step of the way.

Isaiah 40:31

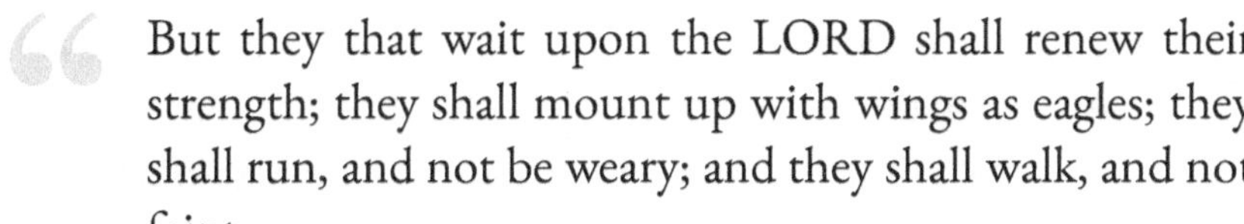

> But they that wait upon the LORD shall renew their strength; they shall mount up with wings as eagles; they shall run, and not be weary; and they shall walk, and not faint.

Parents, in your season of new beginnings, do not grow weary because God will give you the strength to overcome all the trials and tribulations that life brings. As your children grow and learn, you must continue to pray, speak positive affirmations, and keep them covered until they come into the knowledge and understanding of their walk with God. Parents, even though new beginnings bring new challenges, just remember that prayer is one of the greatest tools you can use. Keeping your children lifted in prayer on a daily and consistent basis, you cannot go wrong because God knows what is best for each of them, even though they are all different and are all on different paths in life. Parents, sometimes new beginnings can feel like you are starting life all over again because you are in a new place in life with yourselves and with your children, but most of all, you are in a better place in your walk with God. Starting over is never easy, especially when it is hard to accept change, but new beginnings will allow you to be open to far greater options because you know that you will not go back to the way you used to do things.

It gives you the opportunity to be more open-minded and to rethink the way you see and do things by allowing God into your open-mindedness, the way you think, and the way you do things. Parents, this way, you can now go to God for help when you need to make any choices or decisions, whether it is for your children or yourselves. New beginnings will bring new growth for the parents and the children; growth will allow the parents to see their progress with their children. Growth allows you to see how far you have come and how far you need to go because, with children, the growth process never stops, even when they are older. Parents, your children need to know that you are in their corner to let them know when they are wrong or right and whether they have made the wrong or right decision. Children rely on their parents for many things, even if they do not think you understand where they are in life. Parents, your children are trying to find their place in life. They want to know where they fit in. They are faced with many temptations in life, and they are exposed to so many different things, both good and evil, and they do not always make the right choices.

Parents, the devil has tried to make your children his prime targets. Many children have become so rebellious, disobedient, and smart at the mouth, which makes them wide open for the devil to target them. The exposure that children get nowadays is extremely crazy, and you wonder why your children are acting so crazy. The devil has divided the family with so many evil devices and schemes. The devil is trying to destroy the world through technology; everything is moving at a rapid pace, and your children are caught smack dead in the middle of it all. Parents do not get lost are caught up with Satan and his evil devices. Remember, Satan wanted to take God's place and rule heaven and earth, but the word of God tells us in.

Psalm 24:1

> The earth is the LORD's, and the fullness thereof; the world, and they that dwell therein.

Parents, Satan wants to control the minds of your children. He wants to tell them what to think, what to do, and how to behave. So, parents, this is why it is so important that you are focused and in tune with what is happening in your children's lives. This is why it is important that you pray over your children and cover them with the blood of Jesus because Satan, the devil, is out lurking for his next victim. Sometimes, parents must fast and pray for their children because they have no idea that some of the things they have gotten themselves into are the traps they have walked into. But as praying parents, God will allow you to see the tricks, tactics, and schemes that the devil will use others to lower your children in. Parents, there will be times when your children will not understand the things you tell them to stay away from due to the harm that it would cause but sometimes telling them is like talking to a brick wall. The very things you warn your children about are the things that the enemy uses to tempt them with most, but parents, do not worry because, on your journey of new beginnings, the enemy will do things to tempt you to give up on your children. This is when you must speak the word of God against every temptation, lie, and defeat that the enemy will send your way.

 The thief cometh not, but for to steal, and to kill, and to destroy I come that they might have life, and that they might have it more abundantly.

The enemy will do anything to steal your joy and your peace, but God will give you the strength to overcome it all. Parents, the enemy, do not want you to start fresh with new beginnings because the enemy wants to keep you and your children living in the past. This is why you must stay in the word of God and remain prayerful so you can identify the tricks and schemes of the enemy. Parents, new beginnings give you the opportunity to take a fresh breath and move differently in life, getting rid of the old and welcoming the new. Parents, your children will not see things the way you do because children tend to see things from their view of life, the way they think things in life should be. But it is okay because as you continue to teach them along this life journey, they will grow and develop a better understanding of the things that they are being taught. Parents, teaching your children God's word is very crucial because Satan is pushing his evil agenda on your children. The enemy's job is to point your children in the wrong direction because children nowadays have a lot of mouths on them, and they have a hard time following what their parents are teaching. But if you trust God, he will bring it all together at His timing, and remember, God's timing is not on your watch.

Parents, when God is at work in your children's lives, you must allow him to do things his way and not your way. One thing about God is that he never rushes His process; sometimes, his process happens quickly, and sometimes, it takes a longer period than you anticipated it to be, but remember, God is not on your timing. Parents, not all children are apt to learn new teachings or eager to accept change, so God must take his time with them by taking them through a longer process. That longer process is called life lessons. Sometimes, God must go in and tear down those strongholds, walls, and barriers that your children have put up due to the pain they had to endure, and we all know that sometimes pain can make you bitter. These are some of the things that God must remove from your children's lives for them to move forward in their new beginnings. Remember, parents, new beginnings bring new challenges, but God can handle them all. Parents, for your children to know and trust God, it is a process. God will allow your children to go through things in life so he can bring them out. Once they know that God will bring them out, this will help to build their confidence and trust in God more. Parent, God knows your children, and he knows what it would take to get them to where they need to be in life.

Parents, at some point in life, your children must decide to choose God for themselves because, as parents, you can only take them so far in life. They need to know God for themselves. Parents, your children are smart and intelligent; they can learn a lot on their own. That is why it is so important to teach them about God and his word: as parents, you should instill in your children that which is everlasting. God will never fail, and his word will never return to Him void.

Isaiah 55:11

> So shall my word be that goes forth from my mouth; it shall not return to me void, but it shall accomplish what I please, and it shall prosper in the thing for which I sent it.

Parents, if your children have no knowledge of God or His word, then they would not know who God is or what the Scripture says. Parents children do not always want what is best for them, so you must find ways to encourage them to do what is best for them, not just for the present moment but for what will carry them throughout life itself. Life is a journey that no one knows where it will take them, but one thing is for sure: you should never take life's journey without God, the creator of all things, the one who knows everything about you. Children are innocent; they learn what you teach them, and they apply it to their everyday lives. What they see and learn is what they do. So, parents, in your new beginnings, you can be more creative in the way you would like to see the directions that your children are going, even though God orders their footsteps. God still gives the parents the authority to make their own decisions for their children until they are old enough to do so for themselves. As children grow older, they want to make their own decisions, but there will come times when parents must correct their decision-making because children do not always know what is best for them.

God gave parents the responsibility to raise their children, to teach, lead, and guide them through life until they can care for themselves. So, parents, what you teach them is what they will take with them on their life journey. In your new beginnings, you have an opportunity to give your children some great nuggets from the word of God that will carry them into eternity if they apply it to their everyday lives. Parents, I know sometimes it seems as if it goes in one ear and comes out of the other, but they are listening because they will later remind you what you told them. That way, you will know that they were listening to you the whole time. Parents, your children have a great understanding; they just choose what they want to understand at that moment, but they hear you. Children are special human beings that will grow up to become great men and women. So, parents, whatever you instill in them is what they will carry on. Parents, what you teach your children will either help them take the right or the wrong path in life; that is why it is so important that you teach your children about God and his word. Because at some point in life, every human being will have to seek God for themselves. Teaching them from a child gives them a better understanding of knowing that trying to do life without God is impossible, but with God, all things are possible. If parents can teach their children how to obtain secular knowledge, surely, they can teach them how to obtain godly knowledge. Just knowing the word of God and applying it to your everyday life can save you from a whole lot of trouble. It will not stop trouble from coming your way, but it will help you overcome the troubles that come your way.

James 1:2-4

> Consider it pure joy, my brothers, and sisters, whenever you face trials of many kinds because you know that the testing of your faith produces perseverance. Let perseverance finish its work so that you may be mature and complete, not lacking anything.

Parents teaching their children the word of God will prepare them to put their trust in God by totally depending on him because most children depend on their parents their whole childhood up to a young adult and for some even longer into their adult life. Parents, your children need to know how to let go of depending on their parents and turn to God with one hundred percent of their trust in God and depend on him wholeheartedly. So, parents, in your new beginnings, your focus should be on leading and directing your children to God because your new beginnings will bring on a better meaning in life. These new beginnings will bring change to the parents and the children's lives. Parents, you are never too old to learn, and your children are never too young to learn. Parents' lives may bring on many challenges, but together, you all as a family can overcome them all because God will see you through them all. Spending time with God will make a big difference in your lives.

Parents Speak Affirmations Over Your Children

My children are the head and not the tail. Above and not beneath. Deuteronomy 28:14

My Children can do all things through Christ, who strengthens them. Philippians 4:13

My children are the righteousness of God through Christ Jesus. II Corinthians 5:21

My children are free because they that the son set free is free indeed. John 8:36

My children walk in the favor of God. Psalm 84:11

My children shall be like a tree planted by the rivers of water that bringeth forth their fruit in due season. Psalm 1:3

My children walk by faith, not by sight. II Corinthians 5:7

My God shall supply all my children's needs according to his riches in glory by Christ Jesus. Philippians 4:19

My children love not the world neither the things that are in the world. I John 2:15

My children abide in God, and God's word in them, and whatever they ask of him it is done unto them. John 15:7

My children being confident of this very thing, that he which hath begun a good work in them will perform it until the day of Jesus Christ. Philippians 1:6

God create in my children a clean heart, O God; and renew a right spirit within them. Psalm 51:10

My children trust in the LORD with all their heart, and they lean not unto their own understanding. In all their ways, acknowledge him, and he shall direct their path. Proverbs 3:5-6

My children seek ye first the kingdom of God, and his righteousness; and God will add all these things unto them. Matthew 6:33

My children study to show themselves approved unto God a workman that needeth not to be ashamed, rightly dividing the word of truth. II Timothy 2:15

My children pray without ceasing. I Thessalonians 5:17

My children know that the thief cometh not, but for to steal, and to kill, and to destroy, but that God came that they might have life and that they might have it more abundantly. John 10:10

My children lift their eyes unto the hills from whence cometh their help, for their help cometh from the Lord, which made heaven and earth. Psalm 121:1-2

Parents, God is a God of His word. Numbers 23:19 says God is not a man, that he should lie, neither the son of man, that he should repent: hath he said, and shall he not do it? Or hath he spoken, and shall he not make it good?

PARENTS, USE THIS SPACE TO WRITE YOUR AFFIRMATION.

Parents Pray Over Your Children

Father God, in the name of Jesus, I lift my children up to you (add your children's name), and I pray that you would keep them in the palm of your hands. God leads and directs them every step of the way. God, I pray your favor and protection over their lives, God, cover them and show them the way, God; I pray that they will walk upright before you. God, you said in your word that you would never leave them nor forsake them. God, I pray that you will go before them and be with them no matter where they are in Jesus' name. Amen.

God, you said in your word, Proverbs 22:6, to train up a child in the way they should go, and when they are old, they will not depart from it. Father God, as a parent, I pray that you will bless me with the wisdom and knowledge to teach my children the right way of living. God help me to teach them with understanding and not allow them to lead themselves so when they grow old, they will not forget what they have been taught. Amen.

Father God, in the name of Jesus, I pray that my children will not go through life believing that they can do life on their own because, according to Philippians 4:13, Your word says, I can do all things through Christ which strengthened me. God helped them realize that without You, they could do nothing, but through You, they could do all things. In Jesus' name, Amen.

Heavenly Father, Jeremiah 29:11 says, For I know the plans I have for you, declares the LORD, plans to prosper you and not to harm you, to give you hope and a future. God, no matter what my children must face in this life, despite the hardships or the suffering, you promise that you have a plan to prosper them and give them hope despite their current circumstances. God, I pray that my children will walk according to the plans that you have for their lives. In Jesus' mighty name Amen.

Father God, I pray that my children would choose their friends wisely. Proverbs 18:24 tells us, A man that hath friends must show himself friendly, and there is a friend that sticks closer than a brother. Father God, I pray that you bless my children and give them true godly friends who will correct them through love when they are wrong and encourage them to do the right thing. God, I pray that you would protect them from those who would lead them astray through negativity, bad behavior, and conflict; God bless them with friends who love them and want what is best for them, and they do the very same for them in Jesus most holy name I pray Amen.

Heavenly Father, I pray that you would bless my sons and daughters with true godly wives and husbands because you said in your word, Matthew 19:6 wherefore they are no more twain but one flesh. What therefore God hath joined together let not man put asunder. Father God, bless their marriage to be holy and without blemish unto you, God. Father God, let no human being break their marriage covenant. God let my daughters be submitted unto their husband with respect unto them and let my sons love their wife as their own body because he loves his wife and loves himself. In Jesus' mighty name, I pray, Amen.

Parents, whatever prayer God lays on your hearts to pray, let the Holy Spirit lead you because all children are different; therefore, their needs are different. Parents do not let your prayer life stop here; prayer is an ongoing thing. There will be times when you will have to pray for other children; just remember, it takes a village to raise children.

PARENTS, JOT DOWN THE PRAYERS YOU WOULD PRAY OVER YOUR CHILDREN DAILY.